LISTENING TO URBAN KIDS

*School Reform and the
Teachers They Want*

Bruce L. Wilson
and H. Dickson Corbett

State University of New York Press

Published by
State University of New York Press, Albany

© 2001 State University of New York

All rights reserved

Printed in the United States of America

For information, contact State University of New York Press, Albany, NY
www.sunypress.edu

Production by Dana Foote
Marketing by Anne Valentine

Library of Congress Cataloging-in-Publication Data

Wilson, Bruce L.
Listening to urban kids : school reform and the teachers they want /
Bruce L. Wilson and H. Dickson Corbett
p. cm. — (SUNY series, restructuring and school change)
Includes bibliographical references and index.
ISBN-13: 978-0-7914-4839-7 (hardcover : alk. paper) —
978-0-7914-4840-3 (pbk. : alk. paper)
ISBN 0-7914-4839-8 (alk. paper) — 0-7914-4840-1 (pbk. : alk. paper)
1. Education, Urban—Pennsylvania—Philadelphia—Case studies.
2. Middle school students—Pennsylvania—Philadelphia—Interviews.
3. Educational change—Pennsylvania—Philadelphia.
I. Corbett, H. Dickson, 1950–
II. Title. III. Series.

LC5133.P5 W55 2001
370'.9748'11—dc21
00–063577

10 9 8 7

CONTENTS

ONE

INTRODUCTION

The premise of this book is a simple one: If substantial reforms to improve what and how much students learn actually occur in schools, then students' descriptions of their classroom experiences should reflect those changes. Reform, in other words, should become noticeable in what students say about school.

For example, a central feature of most urban education reform initiatives these days is increasing students' sense of belonging at school and, thereby, their commitment to coming to and working at school. It should be heartening, then, to hear a student explain that she was getting a good education in the following way, as one from the study on which this book is based did:

> My teacher know how to talk to you, like when you having a problem. Instead of having a temper or nuttin', they just be nice. You can go to them and ask a question. They just don't want to hurry you up and get you out of they class.

Similar comments from a sizeable number of students could lead one to assume that such changes as looping, schools within a school, respect training, and the like had taken hold and woven themselves productively into daily school life.

On the other hand, if after having made those changes and emphasized their importance for several years, educators heard an equal number of students still making statements such as the ones below (again, as our study participants did), then they may want to revisit the strategies they are using to create a feeling of belonging.

> My other teacher is always saying: "Didn't you hear me!? Didn't you hear me!? I'm not repeating it!"

> I think teachers should treat all (students) equal, but they
> treat some like better. If a kid do something wrong, the
> teacher treat him like bad and don't care about him; and then
> will treat another kid like he the world. The teacher like one
> student better than the other.

The students, of course, may be blithely unaware of intentional
investments in planning and training intended to enable their teachers
and administrators to act differently and, thus, may gaze blankly at direct
inquiries about "the Goals 2000 initiative," "Success for All," or, in our
case, Philadelphia's "Children Achieving." But regardless of students'
familiarity with the particulars of a reform, their accounts of what they
and their teachers do in class should serve as indications of whether the
reform has penetrated to the classroom level. These indications, while
not carrying the political weight of supposed "objective" measures like
standardized test scores, should provide a school system with valuable
information about whether changes in test scores accurately reflect any
substantive changes in teaching and learning.

Acknowledging the merit of this proposition, the Philadelphia Education Fund (PEF)—with funding from the Pew Charitable Trusts—
supported a three-year study of students in five Philadelphia middle
schools. (A sixth was added in the last year of the study for reasons
detailed later.) The five served some of the city's poorest neighborhoods
and had long histories of poor attendance and low achievement. The
research plan was to select a representative cohort of fifty sixth graders
from each building to follow through their middle school years. PEF
would use the interviews conducted in the spring of each year as one of
several contributions to its efforts to supply feedback to the District about
its reform progress.

We fully understand that in this age of accountability students'
depictions of their classroom experiences will not be widely accepted as
compelling evidence of reform's impact. The use of standardized test
scores as a proxy for school quality has become too common a feature of
the educational landscape for us to be so naïve to think otherwise. Still,
we would argue, the converse should be true as well. If test scores improve
without students noticing much different in school, then people would
be justified in regarding the supposed quantified improvement suspiciously.

At the time of this study, the Philadelphia School District's accountability system portrayed both good and bad news. The good news was that
student performance in the high poverty sections of the city was showing

signs of significant gains; the bad news was that this performance remained woefully low when compared to the more well-to-do areas inside and outside Philadelphia's boundaries. The students in our study sided with the less sanguine view of the District's efforts. They recounted far too readily and frequently tales of classrooms in which little, if any, learning occurred.

In the following pages, we share these inner-city students' comments about a host of topics that had direct relevance for the status of Children Achieving, and reform in urban schools in general. In chapter 2, we address the changes students said they had seen during the three years—in their educational plans and experiences, their schools, and their classrooms. The extent of the changes were identified in two ways: (1) having students in the third year reflect on any differences in their experiences that were obvious to them and (2) comparing what students said about their classrooms, teachers, and classmates from one year to the next. On the whole, continuity rather than change was the norm.

Chapter 3 highlights the students' descriptions of the differences in pedagogy, subject content, and learning environment they experienced as they moved from classroom to classroom. The magnitude of within-school variations in these critical aspects of school functioning was the most startling product of the interviews. It was not unusual for a student to move from a classroom exemplifying the best in urban education to one reflecting the worst in the brief span of a five-minute class change-over.

We emphasize in chapter 4 the value of students as constructive education critics. Students vividly portrayed not only the teachers they wanted to avoid if they could but also the ones they desperately wanted to have. That chapter is the heart of this book. It attends to the teacher actions that students reported as best improving the level of their learning—most notably:

- Pushing students to complete assignments
- Maintaining order
- Being willing to offer help whenever and for however long it was needed
- Going to great lengths to explain assignments and concepts
- Varying classroom activities
- Respecting students and their outside-of-the-school worlds

Students seemed to be saying that they most highly valued teachers who refused to allow them to fail and rendered harsh judgment on those who

<u>did not</u>. They recognized that they gave teachers many excuses for giving up on them. The teachers who taught them best did not accept these excuses. In the process, the most valued teachers came across as strict, even annoyingly so, but, as one student argued, they did so because "the whole point of it is to keep you from failing."

The fifth chapter discusses students' experiences in a sixth middle school. It troubled us that after the first two years of the study we could detect little that had changed in the five schools. While we had no reason to discount the accuracy of students' comments, it was possible that either our original premise or our style of talking with students was not suitable for the purpose of using students as windows through which to view a reform's evolution. Thus, PEF supported fieldwork in another site, one that had already been working closely with a major research and development (R&D) center as one of its pilot demonstration schools. The R&D center sought to create a "strong learning" environment in urban schools through intensive staff development and a challenging curriculum in the core subjects. Available research indicated that the school had implemented certain changes that should have made its educational program markedly different from the ones in the other five schools, even though the school was demographically similar (see, for example, MacIver, Balfanz, & Prioleau, 1999). We felt, therefore, that including eighth graders from this school would give us a better basis for judging the value of using student talk as windows into reform.

Our efforts were rewarded. The students in the school painted a much more balanced and brightly hued portrait of their educational experiences, imbued with greater instructional consistency and more uniform expectations for student performance than we heard about in the other schools. These additional students, thus, not only boosted our confidence in the research strategy, but also lent considerable credence to the suggestions of students in the five schools about how to have a positive impact on learning.

Finally, we reflect on two topics in chapter 6: (1) the implications of the students' descriptions and insights for educational reform, and (2) the value of using students as sources of feedback on the progress of reform. Ultimately, we conclude that for reform to be successful it has to touch students' classroom lives **noticeably**—and students are in the best position to let us know that this has occurred.

The remainder of this chapter provides some brief background about the reform context in Philadelphia during the 1995–1998 school years, our rationale for using students' descriptions as indicators of the impacts of reform, and an overview of the study and the participating schools.

THE REFORM CONTEXT

Philadelphia seemed to provide an appropriate reform context for using students' comments as windows through which to view reform. Both symbolically (Children Achieving was the umbrella label for a package of changes) and substantively (through committing a major portion of the reform's resources to classroom-focused activities), the District emphasized student behavior and performance as the primary targets of reform. In addition, the initiative had been launched two years prior to the study's beginning and increased in its organizational and political intensity during the three years of the study. Thus, it was entirely reasonable for us to expect that by the end of our study—five years into the reform— we would begin to see classroom-level effects showing up in students' descriptions of what they did each day in school.

According to the District (Philadelphia School District, 1999), through Children Achieving, Philadelphia's administrators, teachers, and staff:

1. "Set high expectations for all children and all schools."
2. "Developed tough, new standards, more effective teaching methods and better ways to hold ourselves accountable."
3. "Found ways to make the system 'feel' smaller and more user-friendly."
4. "Expanded teacher and leadership training dramatically."
5. "Expanded full-day kindergarten programs to every child in Philadelphia."
6. "Broadened and reinforced the safety net for children."
7. "Increased student access to books and computers and build and renovated schools."
8. "Engaged the public as partners in school improvement."
9. "Vigorously pursued more adequate and equitable resources and worked to use them effectively."
10. "Instead of choosing among these strategies to improve our schools, we have pursued all of them at once—and for a sustained period of time."

These ambitious and costly steps hoped to break the decades-long history of student failure in the city.

Philadelphia's then-new superintendent launched Children Achieving in 1993 in an atmosphere charged with cynicism about the prospects of accomplishing much of substance with the District's more than 200,000 students. However, the effort received a much-needed boost from the Annenberg challenge grants. Annenberg invested $500 million in some of the country's largest and most needy school systems (Cervone, 1998), and Philadelphia was one of the first recipients, matching Annenberg's two-for-one offer of $50 million with $100 million from other sources.

This development immediately put the national reform spotlight squarely on urban education. New York City used much of its funding to create small, "excellent schools of choice" (with over 140 having been created by 1999). Chicago, which married an earlier state legislature initiative with the Annenberg challenge, supported small networks of three or more schools and an external partner (such as a community group, nonprofit organization, cultural institution, or university) to improve teaching and learning. Philadelphia initially concentrated these modest resources (by large-city standards) on several clusters composed of a high school and its attendant feeder elementary and middle schools and eventually shifted its focus to the entire district. While reform observers like Shields and Knapp (1997) caution that the most promising systemic reforms tend to have a more modest scope, the District faced overwhelming political and educational pressure to extend Children Achieving to benefit all children. Thus, all six of the schools in which we interviewed students were a part of Children Achieving. However, only the one that partnered with the R&D center received significant resources beyond what most schools in the District got to engage in reform activities.

By 1998, the District reported progress implementing several of the structural and organizational elements of its reform plan. These included the institution of school clusters within the district and small learning communities (SLC) within buildings (Christman, Foley, Passantino, & Mordecai-Phillips, 1998), the development of a system of performance indicators (Luhm, Foley, & Corcoran, 1998), and the establishment of instructional standards (Simon, Passantino, & Foley, 1998)—all three of which were in tune with changes being advocated widely around the country. The District's administration felt that the SLC arrangement facilitated school-based decisionmaking, collegial sharing, and students' sense of belonging. In response to heated criticism of the accountability measures from both inside and outside the system, the school board commissioned an external review by a panel of educational assessment experts. This panel basically approved of the system, offering only a few minor suggestions for revision. The standards, the District believed, brought coherence to a rambling, patchwork curriculum that had been decades long in the making.

Corresponding gains in students' standardized test scores encouraged the District to continue on its reform path, and, despite perennial funding shortages, in the fall of 1998 the District announced another set of changes directly aimed at improving these student results further. Staying in touch with national trends, the District proposed ending all vestiges of social promotion and raising the standards necessary for students to move on to higher grade levels. Recognizing that increasing expectations without correspondingly enriching the instructional support for inner-city students would be a hollow and futile endeavor, the superintendent stated that more would be demanded of students only if additional funds for professional development, staffing, and curriculum were forthcoming from the Pennsylvania State Department of Education.

Despite this acknowledgment that the District's schools needed more resources to reform successfully, the schools found themselves in a high-stakes accountability environment. Efforts to reconstitute the staff of a couple of low-performing schools engendered impassioned support and resistance. Although reconstitution was rare, its threat continued to hang over the schools whose students had a long history of failure, including the schools in our study.

None of the five middle schools chosen to be in the study originally received resources for reform above and beyond what other schools got. They all immediately reorganized themselves into SLCs, although in most instances this change amounted to re-labeling already existing "houses." Both teachers and principals in each school participated in mandatory staff development geared toward creating instructional environments that promoted learning, jointly devised school improvement plans to serve as their blueprints for change, and girded themselves for the onset of the District's accountability system that was anchored by a heavy dose of standardized testing in the spring of each year.

One could have argued, convincingly and correctly, that the available resources and strategies were too scattered and weak to be expected to have much substantive impact. Children Achieving, however, had the political backing of all the major players in education in Philadelphia, including the teachers, administrators, school board, business community, and charitable organizations. Thus, the reform had considerable symbolic punch and consequently insinuated itself into adults' discussions about education in Philadelphia. Our goal was to see if the initiative had insinuated itself into students' comments about instruction.

STUDENTS AS USEFUL WINDOWS THROUGH WHICH TO VIEW REFORM

When we discussed the study with teachers in the participating schools, they expressed keen interest and issued nervous chuckles about what we might hear students say. Students, they feared, might avail themselves of this opportunity to offer vigorous and unbalanced complaints about their teachers and schools. The interviews then would become gripe sessions and, worse, lead to yet more public criticism of the District's schools. Despite their inextricable daily physical bond with students, the adults found themselves questioning what students could say that would be relevant to their work. Such a belief apparently is not unusual among teachers (Heshusius, 1995). Still, to their credit, the teachers recognized their concerns as merely hypotheses and were willing for us to have unrestricted access to whichever students became part of the research.

We had had prior experience with listening to students talk about school and were already convinced that their perspectives would be both simply stated and profoundly penetrating (Corbett & Wilson, 1995). A vibrant, though thin, thread of research on students' lives in classrooms burgeoned our confidence. Indeed, long ago, Jackson (1968) established the value to educational thinkers of immersing oneself in the day-to-day life of schools. Seeing what students did and listening to what students had to say about what they did provided bountiful grist for the mill of uncovering, depicting, and critiquing patterns of schooling. However, the primary value of the students' role in such research resided in the increased credence it lent to the researcher's voice in educational thought.

Recent researchers have centered students more directly as articulate and—in their own way—sophisticated observers of school life. For example, Nieto (1994) cogently argued that although some youth, particularly minority adolescents, were alienated from the institution of school and attached no worth to adults' expectations for "good" students, they were yet able to articulate the events, circumstances, and interactions that influenced their construction of this perspective. With such students, enacting higher standards, alternative modes of assessment, or more attractive opportunities to learn would not yield much success until the root causes of their disaffection found their way to the surface of educational discourse. Adults, therefore, would have to become well-versed in these adolescents' worlds—and how to connect to them—as a prelude to embarking on new designs for how to operate schools.

Poplin and Weeres (1992), in *Voices from the Inside*, described what taking this step looked like in their depictions of the unfolding of a process of discovery in four school communities. As participants wrestled with figuring out the best ways to educate students, they found it productive to engage students in the conversation.

> For it is in coming to know that we came to want to act. It is in the listening that we were changed. It is in the hearing our own students speak, as if for the first time, that we came to believe. (1992:19)

To involve students in this way required that the adults recognize them as legitimate participants in educational debate rather than as mere beneficiaries of adults' ministrations, to use Fullan's (1991) distinction. The authors detailed how student input at the improvement table heightened participants' understandings about a range of topics, including relationships, race/culture/class, values, teaching and learning, safety, and the physical environment. Poplin and Weeres concluded that both the quality of and the commitment to the eventual actions taken in the sites benefited immeasurably from students' participation.

Oldfather (1993) and Oldfather and West (1999) reported on a line of research that had students serving as co-researchers in describing the kinds of classroom experiences that motivated them to want to learn to read. The students' conclusions went well beyond mere feedback to their teachers as the teachers turned these perspectives into deliberate actions to promote "meaningful" learning. The students, therefore, became co-constructors of pedagogical practices that helped them learn best, much as Michie's (1999) students did in his self-report of learning to teach in an urban setting. In the process, students became more empowered to take control of their learning and teachers became more effective in facilitating learning.

In *Kids and School Reform*, Wasley, Hampel, and Clark (1997) elevated student voice to the level of schoolwide reform. The authors ventured into schools that were participating in the Coalition of Essential Schools with the expressed purpose of correcting an oversight in reports on the direct effects of reform—students. Through their extended conversations over several years, they were able to track how the particular journey each school took specifically affected six individuals. Vignettes about the students succinctly highlighted the features in the schools that eventually promoted the greatest in-school success: connecting established classroom routines with an expanded instructional repertoire; exhibiting caring for individual students and demanding excellence of all of them; balancing a rigorous adherence to standards with an unending search for innovative ways to enhance student learning; and creating small enough, meaningful units within the building that facilitated widespread discussions among students and adults.

Fully convinced of the value of listening to students as an important part of planning, implementing, and adjusting reform, we sought to extend this line of research to a larger cohort of middle school students, with periodic feedback points to the schools and District built in (see Corbett & Wilson, 1997a; Corbett & Wilson, 1997b; and Wilson & Corbett, 1999). Our overall purposes in conducting the study were to document students' perceptions of their educational experiences and to track how these perceptions evolved over a three-year period. Both we and PEF knew that the proof of Children Achieving would ultimately reside in increased student success in school—greater participation, higher achievement, and strengthened ability to direct their own learning in the future. Objective proof would likely be a long time coming. In the shorter term, it seemed worthwhile to see if something in students' school lives was going on that could give an indication as to what the District might expect in the way of results. Our assumption was that if this "something" was substantial, then we would hear it in students' descriptions of classroom activity.

OVERVIEW OF THE STUDY AND ITS PARTICIPANTS

PEF initially selected five schools to participate, primarily because these served some of the poorest neighborhoods in the city and had been among the lowest performing on standardized measures of student achievement. In the final year of the study, a sixth school was added. This school, with a comparable student population, had additional resources to implement the District's reforms, including the partnership with the R&D center. The partnership had yielded several curriculum and instruction changes that were not yet apparent in the original five schools. Because one of the most remarkable parts of our interviews in the five original sites over the first two years was the consistency of students' accounts about what went on in classrooms, we worried that such descriptions may not have been as sensitive to reform as we had originally thought they would be. Thus, including students who had clearly encountered different content and pedagogy would give us a better idea about the value of student talk as an indicator of reform's penetration to the classroom level.

The Student Sample and Interview Strategy

Each school selected fifty sixth graders to be interviewed. The schools varied in how they handled this task. One principal actually used the computer to randomly generate the list; two others turned the assignment over to the school's' roster person; and the other two asked each SLC coordinator to identify a set of students. We emphasized our wish that the students reflect diversity in instructional experience, academic performance, behavior, motivation, gender, and race—proportional to the overall student populations in each school. Because the schools would remain anonymous to any groups beyond our funding agency and ourselves, they had little need to "stack the deck." In getting to know the students, we had no sense that one segment of the student population was under or overrepresented. Schools notified students according to their established procedures, and each year we gave students the option of not participating when we actually showed up to interview them. Only a couple ever declined.

We interviewed the students individually in the spring of the year, usually for thirty to forty-five minutes. Each of us interviewed the same students over the three years, spending approximately an equal amount of time in the buildings. We talked to 247 sixth-grade students the first year. We could never track down three of the original 250—either they happened to be sick when we tried to contact them, had just been suspended, or had been spotted in the building but were not presently in the classroom they were scheduled to be in. By the third year, 172 (70 percent) of them were still available for interviews. Each year's attrition was mostly due to transfers within or outside the system. Of these 172 on the rolls in 1998, we interviewed 153, the remainder being, once again, either enrolled but chronically absent, enrolled but suspended, or enrolled and in school but too elusive to locate.

Also in the first year we interviewed a set of 114 eighth-grade students. We wanted to guard against the possibility that our sixth graders would note changes two years hence that were more the product of adolescent maturation and development than school improvement. This proved to not be of consequence, as the eighth graders' collective accounts of their experiences were indistinguishable from the sixth graders'—both quantitatively in terms of the number of times students made a particular response and qualitatively in terms of the types of responses they made (see Corbett & Wilson, 1997a, for more on this point).

We developed the original interview protocol with input from PEF and school staff members. It is reproduced in the Appendix. Questions in subsequent years reflected important issues that emerged from the prior year's answers and, therefore, took the form of probes, asking students to explain what they had meant by previous comments, to describe if, how, and why a particular comment still applied to the current year, and to provide examples of their observations. We also tried to take advantage of the interests and concerns students brought up each year. Thus, the exact questions we used increasingly varied from student to student. The interviews were free-flowing, often resembling a conversation—with an unwavering focus on students' learning experiences and how they felt about them.

As middle-aged Caucasian males familiar with Ogbu's penetrating analyses of the subtexts of interracial relationships in schools (see, for example, Fordham & Ogbu, 2000), we wanted to disrobe ourselves of as much of the cloak of authority as we could. We quite naturally worried that students would regard us suspiciously and, therefore, would be circumspect with their answers. Our uneasiness increased because from the beginning of the study we were able to move about freely in the rambling buildings, unescorted and unidentified beyond signing in, and never once had our presence questioned—this in a time of heightened concerns about school security. Our conclusion was that people figured that two casual but neatly dressed, strange white men wandering about in inner-city schools had to be on "official" business.

We took several steps in an attempt to appear less official. First, we would ask students directly if they wanted to do an interview and when it would be convenient to do so. Not surprisingly, most students were reluctant to give up lunch and free time to talk. Respecting their choice of class periods necessitated our getting individual teachers' permission as well. While this strategy meant that we spent a good bit of time locating students and making arrangements ourselves, it gave us the opportunity to wander the halls and garner snippets of what the classes students described in the interviews looked and sounded like.

Second, we conducted the interviews in various places around the buildings—the back of an auditorium, a bench in a school foyer, a corner of the library, an unused room, a machine shop, a stairwell. We wanted to stay away from the main office suite, avoid being in a place that other students could easily distract us, and offer the student some sense of confidentiality without being hidden.

Third, we took verbatim notes rather than used tape recorders. Our mobile interview strategy would have made using the recorders awkward, but, more important, we thought they would be too intrusive. Students took occasional comfort in the fact that no one other than ourselves could possibly decode our handwriting. The mouth, of course, is quicker than the hand. Our more than twenty years of recording conversations in this way had taught us several rules of thumb that improve the quality of field notes: use an idiosyncratic shorthand to denote the question asked, concentrate on the substantive phrases that follow standard stems (for example, capturing "she takes the time to make sure we understand" instead of beginning with "my teacher helps us a lot because"), throw in an occasional question for which you are not going to record the answer so that you can finish writing the previous answer (for example, "So, who is your favorite basketball player?" or "What do you think of the cafeteria food?"), and asking the student to pause a minute because you want to be sure to get down exactly what was said. Students sometimes would become curious about what we were writing and ask us to read back to them what they had said. Such immediate accuracy checks were helpful and legitimizing.

Data analysis followed a similar pattern each year. We began by reading our respective field notes and writing descriptive memos about emerging themes. We then reread the data to decide on predominant themes and to establish coding categories. For example, the importance of a teacher's being "strict" quickly loomed large in the interviews, which caused us to identify all the different phrases students used to describe this action. Our subsequent categorization of the phrases made us realize that students used the term in both a disciplinary and instructional sense, as we will describe in chapter 4. Based on initial coding forays such as this, we would develop data displays of which students in which building made a response. This led to further interpretive memos and discussions. After several revisions, we arrived at the outline that formed the basis of that year's report to PEF. Each of us then went back to our originally coded data to provide additional examples, filling in the outline. This book substantially elaborates the outline used for the third-year report, with occasional insertions from previous years.

We also compared students' descriptions of school life in sixth grade with their final year comments. This was an attempt to see if gradual changes had taken place that were unremarkable to students at any one point in time but were more substantial when viewed across the three years. Such comparisons bore out the students' assessments of little change.

The School Sites

All five of the original schools had veteran principals, and four of these remained in their buildings throughout the study. School #6's principal had been in place for just over a year when we talked with its students and left the following year. The one school with a leadership change—School #5, described below—made one of the more noticeable and positive changes in providing extra help to students during the new principal's second year. All six principals embraced the tenets of the District's reform initiative and worked diligently with their staffs to implement ideas they thought would work for their students. But each school had a character of its own.

School #1. The 1,000 sixth through eighth graders at School #1 were almost exclusively African American (99.3 percent). Relative to the other four schools in the study, these students came from homes that were somewhat better off. Eighty-three percent of the students were from low-income families. The school had a higher daily attendance figure (86 percent) than the other four schools. Students were mostly organized around "pods," with four classrooms sharing a common entry off a rectangular main hall. Students talked of their groups as "pods" rather than small learning communities (SLCs). Students at School #1 usually shared two teachers for their four core academic subjects.

School #2. The 700 seventh and eighth grade students were spread across the top two floors of a five-story building. Our cohort of sixth graders were the last sixth graders to be in the building. Their grade level was exclusively African American. They were split into two groups per grade and rotated among four teachers for their academic subjects within each group. The school had undergone a recent reorganization, resulting in this pattern. Attendance (82 percent) and family income (more than 90 percent low income) were both similar to Schools #3 through #5.

School #3. The largest school in the study, with 1,300 predominantly African Americans (98 percent), spread its students in grades six through eight across five floors. This school had the second highest proportion of suspensions per year (17.6 percent) of the five schools. Students often encountered five different teachers for instruction in their core academic subjects. In fact, thirty-five different teachers worked with the class of eighth graders. The school was organized around seven different SLCs, each with a different occupational focus (for example, hotel and restaurant; law and government; performing arts; etc.).

School #4. Nearly 1,200 fifth through eight grade students attended School #4. This school was the fastest growing, with a reported population of close to 1500 the year after we completed the study. Relative to the other four schools, School #4 had more racial diversity, with two-thirds of the students Latino and the rest African American. Students at School # 4 made almost no mention of their SLCs other than to note that they attended assemblies based on their SLC assignment. Students were enrolled in five core academic subjects and, in most cases, saw three different teachers for those subjects. Unlike the experience of students in School #3 (of comparable size), eight teachers shared the instructional responsibility for the entire eighth-grade class.

School #5. With 660 students, this was the smallest school in the study. It had a predominantly African-American population (86 percent); the remainder were Latino. This school reported the most significant progress on SAT-9 scores during the study and yet was the poorest school with 97.6 percent low income, had the highest suspension rate (34 percent of the enrollment), and served the highest proportion of classified special education students (24 percent). The other schools labeled closer to 10 percent of their students as special education. The five sections of eighth-grade students saw either two or three different teachers for their five core academic subjects. This school also introduced a popular, and apparently effective, after-school program during the last year of our visits, about which more will be said in chapter 2.

School #6. Added in the final year of the study, School #6 was economically similar but demographically more diverse than the other five. Two-thirds of the students were Latino and African American, with the remainder being Asian (mostly from Cambodia and Vietnam) and Arab Americans. Around 85 percent of the students were from low-income families. The most noteworthy difference between School #6 and the others was its participation with the R&D center. The school is the primary subject of chapter 5. We present a much more detailed look at the school there.

OTHER CONSIDERATIONS IN READING THIS BOOK

The main text contains both quantitative data—primarily the percentages of students who made a particular response—and qualitative data, which are illustrative comments from students about various topics. We did not ask every student every question. Some students took longer in answering certain questions, which did not leave enough time to ask others. We occasionally would try out a question on a subset of students to see what sort of response that brought; and, in the final two years, probing questions were based on a student's previous year's responses. Also, students were free to decline to answer anything we asked. This all means that the "Ns" for different sets of responses varied. In each case in which we give the number of students who offered a specific answer, we provide the total number of students asked the question. Students, of course, could give more than one answer to any question. Thus, sometimes "N" refers to the total number of responses students gave rather than the total number of students. We clearly identify such situations.

We rely heavily on student quotes. We feel that their words, not paraphrased by us, are much more powerful and poignant than ours. Moreover, our interest is in portraying the categories students used to characterize their classroom worlds, thereby enabling them to speak more directly to the reader rather than through our more highly abstracted interpretations of their perspectives. Therefore, the text is crammed with quotes.

As we explained earlier, we tried to take verbatim notes as the students talked, and in our excerpts from the interviews, we have remained faithful to the students' syntax and word choices. We did not correct improper grammar nor did we attempt to reconstruct their syntax in places where the students' talking speed exceeded our writing speed. The quotes in the following pages are what students said, with any paraphrases denoted by brackets.

In our feedback sessions to Philadelphia educators, the decision to use students' actual speech patterns received a mixed reaction. Some educators appreciated hearing the students' comments in their own words; they felt it made the statements more concrete, believable, and compelling. Others became distracted with the lack of subject–verb agreement, the portions of verbs students omitted, and mixed tenses. They thought this reflected poorly on the students, themselves, and the District's reform efforts—and would only reinforce global negative assessments of the quality of urban education. We stuck with our original decision.

In excerpts from the interviews, the "I" stands for the interviewer and the "S" for the student. Following each quote is a six-digit number. The first three comprise the student's unique ID; the fourth is nearly always a 6, which denotes that the student was in the original sixth-grade cohort (to distinguish them from the eighth graders interviewed in the first year; comments from these students, though few, have an 8); the fifth is the student's race (1 = African American; 2 = Hispanic/Latino; 4 = Asian; and 5 = Caucasian—these latter two designations were not needed until School #6 was added in the third year; for a while we used a 3 for "other" until we had more than one or two students in the category); and the sixth designates gender (1 = male and 2 = female). While inserting these codes into the text may distract some readers, it provides others with information about a student's demographic characteristics and a way of checking the distribution of the quotes we used.

We use numbers as well for the schools (1–6) and the several teachers discussed in detail (for example, Teacher 1-A or Teacher 1-B). This device, though lacking stylistic merit, provides a way to associate the various student quotes, school examples, and teacher illustrations with one another.

Two

CHANGES IN STUDENTS' SCHOOL LIVES OVER THREE YEARS

Given the type of progress the District reported it had made with Children Achieving, it was not too surprising that our middle school student interviews reflected little in the way of change over the three years. Despite spending an enormous part of their waking hours in school, the students actually saw little of the overall operation of a school district. Changes made beyond the classroom in governance, district-wide assessment strategies, and standards may not have trickled into the daily flow of their school lives, at least not in the short term. Students, therefore, were not well positioned to comment directly and specifically on most of the goals of Children Achieving. We did ask them, however, to think a bit about changes they had seen more generally—in themselves, their schools, and their classrooms. The sections that follow the brief introduction below present their views in detail.

We found that these inner-city middle school students dreamed big. They all planned to go to high school and graduate; most of them expected to go on to college; and nearly all of them anticipated finding employment in their preferred occupational fields. These ideals persisted, and even strengthened, throughout middle school. Indeed, most of the students felt they were well prepared to meet the educational and vocational challenges ahead.

These dreams will likely conflict with reality, if the students' experiences mirror those of most children of poverty. The issue for such children is not ambition so much as execution, knowing how to get from one's goal to the gold, so to speak (see Kusimo, Carter, & Keyes, 1999, as an example). We could detect no great sophistication in our students' understanding of how these dreams could be realized. For students, working hard, getting good grades, and doing what they were told seemed to be the keys to success at all levels of life. Given the formidable economic and social obstacles that inevitably would confront them, these individual traits—however much their teachers might have prized them—would require some embellishment to be effective.

At the school level, we found that students collectively were split about whether changes had occurred. About half noted differences during the three years, primarily in terms of academic and behavioral changes in themselves. It should be pointed out that not all of the students who described such changes indicated that these developments had been for the better. Only a few students singled out organizational and instructional changes they had noticed.

In the classroom, we found that the picture remained essentially the same over the three years: Students defined "good" teachers in the same way and identified dramatic variations in the types and quality of their experiences from classroom to classroom. Nothing, therefore, had dissuaded them from desiring teachers who were willing to help, were strict but nice, and were able to explain tasks and content clearly. At the same time, nothing had happened to alter the spotty distribution of such teachers in their schedules.

The following pages elaborate these changes—or lack thereof—in the students, their schools, and their classrooms, all based on the final year interviews.

CHANGES IN PLANS FOR THE FUTURE

These children—who attended nonmagnet, inner-city schools—often heard that their poor academic performance was mostly a function of their failure to appreciate the value of getting an education. To be fair, the actions of the students—indifferent attendance, casual attention to homework, and frequent misconduct—did little to contradict this argument. The students, however, verbally begged to differ. Almost to a person, they talked confidently of their future plans and education's integral role in helping them realize those dreams. Regardless of the grades they had received to date, the students left middle school fully convinced that they had to complete both high school and college to create a good life for themselves and their families. They valued education.

Moreover, objective measures of their schools' effectiveness to the contrary, students almost universally affirmed that they were ready to do well in high school. Indeed, 82 percent (79 of 96 asked the question) gave a "thumbs up" to their middle school preparation. Only a few argued stringently that they were not prepared. The remaining ones who were not sure that they could handle high school's challenges equivocated, indicating that some of their teachers had done a good job while others had not.

Impressive, too, was the high percentage of students who suggested that they would be going on to college. Ninety percent of them (106 of 117) acknowledged a need for some post-secondary training. This percentage remained remarkably constant over the course of our three years of conversations with the students. The students' aspirations for higher education were equally matched by their positive ideas about their futures. All but a few had specific ideas about what kind of work they would like to do as adults. The vast majority of their vocations required higher education, thus centering education in their occupational paths.

For example, the two most frequently mentioned occupations were doctor ($N = 26$) and professional athlete ($N = 26$). Females mostly mentioned the former while males dominated nominations of the latter. There were also eighteen aspiring lawyers and fifteen cosmetologists, many of whom wanted to own their own business. While not as frequently mentioned, students also talked about being teachers, writers, entertainers, computer specialists, and tradespeople. There was little difference across the five middle schools in the range or popularity of vocations.

Despite three years of modest academic performance in middle school, the vast majority of the students mentioned the same occupations in the eighth grade that they did in the sixth grade. Even the minority who shifted their goals did not necessarily do so in ways that would require less formal education; they were just as likely to pick a job that required more training (for example, secretary to writer or athlete to engineer) or equal training (for example, office worker to barber or teacher to nurse) as they were to shift into occupations with less demanding educational requirements (for example, veterinarian to athlete or nurse to cosmetologist).

We should note too that all of the aspiring basketball and football players acknowledged college as a necessary step; the few dramatic instances of players jumping straight from the schoolyard to professional payrolls had not disavowed them of that notion. Similarly, the hairdressers-to-be did not operate under the illusion that their current skills at braiding hair would translate directly into work without first receiving additional training.

But other than knowing that more education was important, the students had general, simplistic, and almost platitudinous notions about what they would have to do to achieve their desired futures. They either had little idea about what it would take or they fell back on the explanations they offered for what it took to succeed in school: working hard, getting good grades, and staying out of trouble.

We know these virtues sound heartening, and the frequency with which students invoked them as the keys to the future would have surprised teachers mired in the schools' daily disruptive din. From the beginning of our study, students rolled out these phrases as the characteristics of a good student, as the actions that caused a student to be successful, as a plan for graduating from high school, as the tickets to college admission (with only a handful ever mentioning SAT and National Merit scores, class rank, legacies, and other qualities more treasured by college admissions officers), and how one became a professional. Thus, although their advocacy of this triumvirate of success was admirable, their formula seemed to be missing specific ideas about how to put those plans into action.

> S: I still want to go to college.
> I: What will it take for you to get to college?
> S: (*shrugs*) I don't know.
> I: What do your teachers tell you?
> S: They say it good to go to college. (356612)

> Sure I'm gonna finish high school. I have all the qualities—I have confidence in myself and I know I can be anybody. For me, if I try my best, I can do it. (157612)

> It takes hard work to finish college. (261611)

> I don't want a bad life. I want to finish high school and college. I can do that by keeping up my grades and working hard. (369612)

> I'm going to finish high school. To do that, you gotta try hard, really pay attention, or else you won't get the education you need. (467612)

We do not mean to diminish the value of students espousing a "do my best" philosophy. However, their answers seemed overly simplistic solutions to a complex issue. This was especially true given the fact that many of them had admittedly not done their best to date. When asked whether or not they thought they were "on track" to accomplish all they wanted to do in education and work, students were generally quite candid about the need to make some adjustments to their current habits.

S: I'm going to high school and college.
I: Think you will finish both?
S: Yep.
I: What will it take?
S: Good grades.
I: How are your grades now?
S: They're bad, but I'm trying to pull them up.
I: Is that hard to do?
S: I just haven't felt like doing it. (470622)

Just over half of them (generally the ones with lower performance in school) talked about specific changes they would need to make. Students talked about the whats, hows, and whys of changing their approach.

I: Are you on track to meet your goals?
S: No. I need to study more.
I: How do you know that?
S: I just know by some of my grades. [mostly Cs]
I: Why do you think you will be more inclined to do it in high school?
S: I don't want to get let back. I want to go to college.
I: What will you need to do to get better grades?
S: Just do more and more work. I can rest when the school year is over. (123612)

I: Are you on track to accomplish your goals?
S: No, I need to make some changes.
I: What kind of changes?
S: I need to get a better report card. I need to get on the honor roll.
I: What do you need to do to do that?
S: I need to work harder and pass my tests.
I: How do you plan on doing that?
S: I am going to spend more time studying.
I: Why do you think you might take school more seriously in high school than in middle school?
S: 'Cause I want to stay on the honor roll. In high school, it makes you feel good to be on the honor roll because not many are.
I: Are you confident you can get on the honor roll?

S: Yes, because I stayed on the honor roll in elementary [but not in middle school]. (206612)

I: Are you on track to accomplish your goals?
S: No. I need to make some adjustments.
I: Like what?
S: My grades could be better [this is a C student]. I tend to slack off with my friends. Next year I plan to concentrate and focus. My grades will be better.
I: Why are you going to change next year?
S: I just made a promise to myself. I won't let it [getting into trouble] happen. We were in a bloody fight three weeks ago in the lunchroom.
I: What are you going to do differently next year?
S: I plan to be by myself more, concentrate on my goals, and achieve. (211611)

The somewhat unsettling part of this story was the widespread conviction that it would be a very simple matter to turn over a new leaf in high school. Despite poor to average performance and/or less than exemplary social behavior in middle school, most of these students were eternally optimistic that things would be different in high school. What made this disconcerting was both the strong quantitative evidence that these students undoubtedly would perform considerably worse in high school (Furstenberg, Neild, & Weiss, 1998), and the repeated warnings by current teachers that high school teachers would be considerably less tolerant of students' shortcomings. Students said they were told that their high school teachers would assign work and expect its completion, absent the help offered in middle school.

[My teacher] says the high school teachers aren't going to care and keep you [for help]. If you don't do the work, they won't holler at you. They just put an F down. (111611)

Our teacher says that when in high school they won't take any past due assignments like we do. You need to turn things in on time. (126611)

The teachers won't help you as much. You are more on your own. You have lots of work and projects to do. (418622)

In high school they won't take all our fooling around. They are more stricter. They only give you a certain amount of time to get to class. You do your work or you fail. (505611)

So the bottom line was that students had changed little in their plans for the future. This was good news in that students were optimistic about their futures, contradicting most media and some academic portrayals of the apathy and despair associated with urban youth. Indeed, these students did not indicate to us the kind of awareness of social constraints on their future opportunities that Ogbu (1987) argues would lead to little interest in doing well in school. Instead, they seemed to adopt a more meritocratic stance (O'Connor, 1999), envisioning their occupational attainment as a goal within their power to influence.

But there was also bad news. O'Connor (1999) has suggested that minority students who are the most "highly attuned" to barriers to success may in fact achieve the most. Thus, our students' optimism about the ease with which they could adjust their performance and behavior in high school would likely prove to be counterproductive. Essentially they were confident that they could navigate a reportedly less supportive learning environment simply with newfound determination.

In fact, current research shows that 58 percent of freshman in Philadelphia high schools fail at least one course as compared to only 33 percent of eighth graders (Furstenberg, Neild, & Weiss, 1998). Early high school failure is not unique to Philadelphia. Roderick and Camburn (1999) report that over 40 percent of Chicago's ninth graders fail one or more major subjects and that this failure is closely associated with even poorer performance in subsequent years. In that discouraging environment, our students would come face-to-face with the reality of the limits on their post-secondary plans.

Of course, the cynical reader may think that these students had no intentions of going to college or obtaining high-status jobs, that they were simply parroting what they thought we would want to hear. Where was the supposed alienation from middle-class aspirations so often noted in the literature?

We have no way of knowing whether the students we had been in contact with for three years only knew that we would want them to talk about these educational and occupational goals or whether the students both knew about **and** desired these goals for themselves. We were inclined to believe them because nearly everyone spoke in unison. If this population had actually been so disaffected, a few more outspoken ones would have identified themselves. As we will detail later in this chapter and in several others, the students were not at all bashful about criticizing their teachers as instructors. It did not make sense to us, therefore, that they would be so nondiscriminating in discussing education's contribution to their life chances and so discerning in how teacher actions affected their learning without actually meaning it. Moreover, recent research suggests that the relationship between a minority student's self-identity and educational achievement is complex and variable and, thus, cannot be simplistically predicted (Ainsworth-Darnell & Downey, 1998; O'Connor, 1999).

However, for the purpose of figuring out what had changed for students over the three years, the issue of students' forthrightness in this regard really does not matter. The point is that students espoused an ambitious future without ever becoming more sophisticated about how to attain it. We interpreted their general satisfaction with their middle school preparation as a reflection of their certainty that teachers would have only asked them to do the things that would have paved the way for future success in school. Thus, students had received the messages that their teachers probably had wanted them to get—internalized or not. What they had not received very clearly was how to act on these messages effectively.

CHANGES IN THE SCHOOLS

Our discussions with the students about how their schools had changed began with year-to-year comparisons. Three out of five students who engaged in this task (80 of 135) thought some change had taken place, although "changed" did not necessarily mean "better." Changes generally fell into two categories: students having to do more or harder work, and students behaving differently than in previous years. Because students had such apparent difficulty generating examples of specific changes in the schools themselves, we decided to ask a little more pointed question about the SLCs, a cornerstone of the Children Achieving initiative.

More and/or Harder Work

More than a third (29 of 80) of the students who thought changes had taken place felt that they were doing more work than in previous years and/or doing harder work. They offered two reasons for this. The first was that the additional or more difficult work was a consequence of being in eighth grade and its temporal proximity to high school, when for the first time schoolwork really "counted." In the students' minds, eighth grade played a crucial role in facilitating the transition across the grade levels.

> I: Are things at school different or the same when compared to last year?
> S: They are a little different. This is the year that really counts for high school.
> I: What are you doing this year?
> S: The things we do are not just eighth-grade work.
> I: How do you know?
> S: The books are more advanced. The work is more challenging. It is just not that easy. (221612)

> I: Is the work different or the same when compared to last year?
> S: It's different. It's harder. [The teacher] says she is teaching us stuff for high school.
> I: How do you know it's high school work?
> S: She tells us it is. (413622)

> I: Are you learning mostly the same or new things this year?
> S: I'm learning mostly new things. They are getting us ready for high school. They are helping us learn what to expect.
> I: Like what?
> S: Like how to write essays and how to do notetaking. (503612)

The other reason for doing more and/or harder work, particularly for students in School #5, was that teachers and administrators were pushing them to work more than they had in previous years. In most of the buildings, "pushing students" was just another way of saying that the eighth grade was regarded by all as the time to get serious. But, in School #5, the feeling of being continually and forcefully nudged to do work was perhaps more than coincidentally related to the institution of a school-wide, after-school, extra-help and activity program.

School #5's teachers shared the responsibility of staying after school on a regularly scheduled basis to provide additional tutoring and instruction. Of the twenty students who made more than a passing reference to the program, not one dismissed it as unhelpful. Nearly two-thirds of the students (thirteen of twenty) had made an effort to attend; of those who had not, only one hid behind the excuse that he did not know the schedule: "I need it most for math, but I don't know which days [math is taught] or which classroom it is in." (511611) The other six either attended an alternative program elsewhere, had their own private tutor, were needed to deliver a younger sibling home from elementary school, or had a parent fearful of the student's walking home after dark. When asked why this program was started, several students noted that "the principal knew a lot of kids were failing."

The program's routine was highly structured. Students noted that it was much more organized than an occasional, casual visit to a teacher—which had been the hallmark of previous afterschool programs.

> S: You go to the library after school [at 3 P.M.]. All the teachers are waiting for you there [actually teachers took turns depending on the day of the week]. You then go and do schoolwork in the classroom.
> I: What kind of work do you do?
> S: The teacher helps you with your classwork. The whole point of it is to keep you from failing.
> I: What do you do next?
> S: At four forty-five, you go to the cafeteria to get a snack. Then we go to the gym and we get to exercise from five to six.
> I: How many students are involved?
> S: About half of the school. (508611)

The students had to stay for the full three hours and were not allowed to wander around the building at any time. The school, the students observed, wanted them to know they were there to work.

The students went for different reasons, some because they were struggling in a subject and needed the extra help:

> S: I go every day, or at least three times a week. I go for math, English, and computers. I was doing bad (Ds and Fs) in the beginning, but now I am getting Bs and Cs.
> I: Why do you think you are getting better grades?
> S: I started doing the work, you know, completing the assignments.
> I: What prompted you to complete the work?
> S: I wanted to get out of here. (508611)

Others went simply because they really enjoyed the topic and/or found the teacher someone they liked working with:

> S: I go about three times a week.
> I: Why do you go?
> S: To help me learn computers. I do stuff I didn't know how to do.
> I: Is that helpful to you?
> S: Yeah, I have learned new stuff and the teacher helped me. (531612)

> S: I go on Monday and Tuesday. I go because of [teacher's name]. I like the way she teaches math. We are studying algebra [not something they do in the regular class].
> I: How many students come to the class?
> S: About fifteen kids. You know, anyone can come. We just do algebra from about 3:15 to 4:45. (501612)

The key to success of the after-school program, according to students, was that the atmosphere was more conducive to learning. With fewer of their peers around, the students were not as distracted as they were in their regular classrooms and as a result felt that they could put more effort into their work.

> Students are more serious [after school]. They don't got no friends to look at 'em. That way they can work harder. (555611)

> I: Is the after-school program you mentioned a good idea?
> S: Mmhmm.
> I: Why?
> S: It help you a whole lot. It brought my grades back up.
> I: How?
> S: It help me understand.
> I: How many students are there in one class?
> S: Only six or seven and that helps a lot.
> I: Why?
> S: When it's small, you don't have that much people talking, or the teacher banging that stick, so you can go through the work better.
> I: Do you wish your regular classes were like this?

S: Yes, everyone talk too much sometimes. (573612)

I got a F in math first report. So I started going to the "after-school," and I got a D the second report. Now, I got Cs, Bs, and As. When you with friends, you laugh and play. This program helps me understand better what we doing. (553612)

Whatever the reason for their attendance, students reported that this program provided them a way to learn content and study skills that had eluded them during the regular school day.

Different Student Behavior

In noting other changes in their schools, students frequently mentioned changes in student behavior. Although they perceived that adults had tightened their enforcement of the rules and taken additional steps to increase security in the buildings, students were mixed about how effective those changes had been. Some suggested that it improved the general climate of the school.

I: Are things different or the same this year at school?
S: They're different?
I: How are they different?
S: We got to follow harder rules.
I: Like what?
S: No fighting, no running in the halls, be quieter in the lunchroom.
I: Are kids better?
S: Yeah, they are better behaved. (412621)

Others said that implementation of the new measures was spotty, thereby weakening their impact.

S: They've added some extra rules.
I: Like what?
S: If you fight, you get locked up and you can't hang around after 3:30 cause of all the fights.
I: Do the stricter rules work?
S: No.
I: Why not?

S: The NTAs (Non-Instructional Teaching Assistants) don't put more effort into it. At first it worked, but now they just take you to the Dean. (327612)

I: Have there been fewer fights with the new rules?
S: No. They say they will arrest you, but they [students] come right back to class.
I: Are students better behaved?
S: No. (309611)

Small Learning Communities

The schools all reorganized into SLCs. In these, a group of students rotated among a team of teachers, in theory giving both teachers and students the opportunity to know a portion of the school population well. Overall, students rarely commented on this development, possibly because middle schools had begun using a team and/or house concept before the onset of the SLC nomenclature. Indeed, the students made few, if any, observations that could be directly linked to any of the ten goals of Children Achieving that were listed at the beginning of this book. To see if a more concrete reference to one of the aspects of the reform might spur their recollections, we explored the idea of the SLC with a subsample. Their experiences seemed to vary by school, although they clearly associated rather minor alterations in the school routine with the institution of the SLCs and were mixed about whether this reorganization was for the better.

For two of the schools (#1 and #5), students talked about their SLC mostly in the context of field trips that they took. Depending on the SLC, some students reported taking considerably more trips while others lamented only being outside the building once or twice during the year. In a third school (#4), there was almost no mention of the SLCs other than to suggest that they attended assemblies based on their SLC assignment. The fourth school (#2) had undergone a further reorganization that combined students from different grade levels for SLC activities. Students were split on the wisdom of such a move; about half thought it brought fewer fights and more order to the school; the other half found the younger students immature and unwilling to interact constructively. School #3 organized itself around a group of seven different SLCs, each with a different occupational focus (for example, hotel and restaurant; law and government; performing arts; etc.). Students reported more activities related to these occupational themes than the other schools.

For example, one group went on a field trip to learn how a hotel operated, another group performed a stage production for a local senior citizens group, and a third group used the content of law and government to help articulate instruction across their major subjects.

The above discussion does not give an overwhelming sense of change in the middle schools. Remember that a sizeable portion of the students (40 percent) could describe none at all. Thus, asking for year-to-year comparisons and seeking comments about specific elements of Children Achieving were met with the same reaction. The students concisely gave the ubiquitous teenage response to all dinnertime queries about what was new at school that day: "Nothing." But, of course, students spent the majority of their time in classrooms. The next section therefore looks more closely at their depictions of those settings.

CHANGES IN CLASSROOM EXPERIENCES

This book will put a glaring spotlight on teachers. They were the people who had the largest impact on the quality of students' educational experiences. When we pressed students to explain why they regarded a particular experience in a positive or negative light, they laid the praise or blame at teachers' feet. Being a hero or a scapegoat was an unavoidable part of being a teacher in these inner-city schools. For example, in the first year of the study, we asked students, "Are you getting a good education here?" They overwhelmingly said "yes" (almost 75 percent, or 242 out of the combined 330 sixth and eighth graders). Whether students answered "yes," "no," or "somewhat," half of the proffered explanations as to why mentioned teachers. Students themselves were the next most frequently mentioned explanation at 25 percent.

Students were very clear about what they wanted teachers to be like in that first year. They wanted to spend their classroom time in the company of adults who were eager to help students without playing favorites, who were strict but nice and respectful, and who took the time to explain work clearly without becoming tediously repetitive. Slightly more than 75 percent of them mentioned a teacher's being helpful, strict, or able to explain clearly (292 out of 361 interviews). Students' views of their teachers remained constant over the three years, although we will explain in chapter 4 that being strict really had two components: maintaining order in the classroom **and** pushing students to complete their schoolwork.

As attention-getting, at least for us, as the fact that so many students made similar comments was that they made them so often. Offering help when needed, being strict, and explaining well were extensively embedded in the interviews. One or more of these qualities cropped up in numerous places: when students defined a good teacher, offered advice for improving the school, named their favorite classes and explained why, described the daily routines in classes, identified how they learned best, and—perhaps most significantly—compared classrooms in which they learned and behaved to those in which they did not. Students were emphatic in their support of teachers who approximated the ideal, and pleaded for the schools to do something about the others.

Students were so unanimous—and even profound—in this regard that we reserve much of the presentation of these findings to chapter 4 on "Classrooms Students Want." But it is worth offering a brief summary at this point about what students meant by these terms.

A teacher's being willing to help meant that the teacher found a way for the student to get continued explanations of a concept, problem, or assignment until the student understood it. Help took several forms: simply responding to a students' question in front of the entire class; visiting students individually at their desks as they worked on an assignment; suggesting that students with questions "ask three before me" as a way of getting them to view one another as resources; allowing students to work on a task in groups; and being available at nonclass times— before school, after school, or during lunchtime. Different students preferred different ways of getting help, depending on their level of shyness or willingness to admit they were having a problem. The important point was that the help had to result in the students' understanding. Students praised the teacher who "makes sure that I got it," who "makes sure I understand," who "teaches me so I can do it," who "makes it easier to understand," who "makes it clear," who will "actually teach." That was the sole criterion of effectiveness.

This meant that the teacher not only had to be willing to help but also had to be good at explaining. A teacher could be adept at providing explanations in several ways, according to students. First, the teacher broke the concept, problem, or assignment down, and taught it sequentially "step-by-step." Second, the teacher used alternative ways of presenting the material. As examples, students talked about teachers who could tell them what to do and then also "show" them what to do. They applauded teachers who "switch the ways" of explaining and who went over the explanation more than once, using a slightly different variation each time. One student concluded simply that the teacher had to "teach the way we understand." Finally, students described a teacher as good at explaining if they were able to "translate" the material into language more familiar to the students. "Tell me in my own words," more than one student advised.

Then, to succeed, from the students' perspective, teachers had to ignore students' disinterest in the class, their reluctance to tackle a task, and their frequent off-task behavior and teach them anyway. Students did not mean that teachers should overlook such behavior. What they meant was that a teacher could not let such actions defeat him or her. Students said they wanted to learn; they just did not act like it. It fell to the teacher to continually stay on them to do otherwise. Thus, the teacher needed to admonish students, to chide their misbehavior, and to provide fair and appropriate consequences whenever students went too far. Teachers had to be strict, in other words, even in the face of student complaints and apparent preferences to the contrary.

Help until students understand. Explain in the ways they understand. Stay on students until they finish what they now understand they are to do. Students reserved the highest of praise for the teachers who acted like this. Students proclaimed that these were the teachers who "do they job," "teach," "care about us," and "make us learn." These were the teachers students wanted to have.

Such teachers, however, were not evenly distributed throughout the schools. Indeed, one of the primary issues students raised was the abundance of situations in which they felt that they learned little, if anything. Students attributed the root causes of the lack of learning to be the schools' reliance on long-term substitutes—some of whom may have not been adequately prepared and all of whom students regarded as not "regular teachers"—and a host of regular teachers whom students identified as "unable to control the class" or "unwilling to help." None of the schools was immune to the problem of having classrooms in which little learning took place, and nearly every student we talked to experienced the problem firsthand.

Multiple or Long-term Replacement Teachers

More than a few students adamantly asserted that some classes were a "waste." They explained that for some reason—a sabbatical (described by a student as "when you been working for a long time and then take a vacation"), an illness, or simply an abrupt departure ("we got her fired")—their "regular" teacher had left and replaced with a replacement teacher, or a succession of them. In most instances, the consequence was a daily battle between students intent on "sinking a sub" and teachers just trying to get through the day.

S: We had a whole lot of teachers this year.
I: Has that been a good thing or a bad thing?
S: A bad thing.
I: Why?
S: We don't do nothing.
I: What do you mean?
S: We don't do work or nuthin', and they all be acting up.
I: So how has this year been for you?
S: A waste . . . my whole class is going to be retained.
I: How do you feel about being retained?
S: I could do eighth-grade work. They explain the work there. We get split up sometimes [on days when no English teacher shows up] and I went to the eighth-grade class and I could understand it.
I: So how has this year been?
S: We had fun in the beginning [with the regular teacher], but everybody now is failing, except one person. (162612)

Another student, who had transferred out of a class that had had a string of teachers to one that had had the same teacher for the entire year, compared the situations and determined the move had been for the better.

S: Recently I was in [the old section] and I was having problems in that class but I was getting As and Bs so I was transferred to [the top section] . . . they are doing much harder work.
I: What do you mean by harder?
S: It was harder, more reading; in my old section we were getting some work, but in my new section we get more.
I: Could you give an example?
S: The way they do . . . they do definitions different. In my new section you write it, give the abbreviation, break it into syllables, write what part of speech it is.
I: What do students do in your old section?
S: It more like a commercial class; they just there to pass. A lot could do what we do in my new section, it just they are used

> to the easy way instead of working for it . . . they like just sit
> there, do work, the testes [sic] is easy, a little kid could pass.
> I: So you got different work to do in the new section.
> S: [In the old section], we were getting new teachers every
> day and we're not learning, but in my new section my
> teacher gives a test every week. (167612)

Students did not deny that they misbehaved badly when confronted
with a substitute. But students tended to view this as the teacher's in-
ability to control the class. That is, students felt that they were controllable, if the teacher knew how. Nevertheless, the replacements who followed regular teachers into the classroom were definitely in unenviable
circumstances. Thus, the blame for the cumulative "non-educational"
atmosphere undoubtedly should have been shared. The point, however,
is that an entire school year in some core subject areas was, in fact,
wasted. For a student population that collectively achieved well below
grade level, this loss of a year represented a potentially insurmountable
academic gap. The effect was magnified in some schools because students tended to have one teacher for two core subjects. That is, one
teacher taught both science and social studies, or science and math, or
math and language arts. Thus, a student's having multiple teachers or a
long-term substitute could have affected 50 percent of their major
classes.

Disruptive Classrooms

Although the above situations were decidedly disruptive, there also were
instances in which students described difficult learning environments
with their "regular" teachers as well.

> I: What grades are you getting?
> S: As, Bs, and Cs.
> I: What are you getting the C in?
> S: Math.
> I: Is that good or bad for you?
> S: Not a good grade.
> I: Why?
> S: The teacher mostly.
> I: What do you mean?
> S: Like the kids talk, and if one talks, he blame the whole
> class. He screams at us. He threw a desk.

I: Why did you get a C?

S: He did not explain it, and I do poorly on the test.

I: Describe a day in the class.

S: You don't learn nothing. It's boring. He always suspending kids; that's how he wastes his time.

I: Why do kids act up?

S: They don't like the way the teacher acts; other math teachers teach a different subject every week; he teaches the same subject for a month. (468621)

Students not only were willing to note what teachers did wrong but also were ready with pedagogical advice.

I: Are you learning anything in math?

S: No, cause he don't teach us right.

I: What do you mean?

S: He don't teach in his own words. I don't understand. He teach us out of the math book. Whatever he says, he says from the math book and if it is easy, he make it complicated.

I: You want examples?

S: Yes.

I: Do other teachers explain?

S: Yes, they explain it like with little details. (459622)

A seemingly unending cycle emerged in these classrooms. A teacher would discipline the students in ways they did not like. The students, therefore, would continue to misbehave. The teacher would then try to move on through the lesson, often by avoiding interaction with the students. The students' response would be to complain that the teacher was not "really" teaching. The resulting frustration accentuated their misbehavior which in turn caused teachers to try to exert greater control.

"Support scarce" Classrooms

In our conversations, students' expressions of their desire and gratefulness for academic help were prominent. Clearly, students associated whether they were learning with the extent to which the teacher was willing to give help to them. Thus, it was somewhat difficult and artificial to untangle "disruptive" classes from "support scarce" ones. The two often went hand in hand. Still, students stressed the learning benefits of being in "support rich" rather than "support scarce" classrooms.

I: Do you learn more in some classes?
S: Math.
I: Why do you say that?
S: Cause he explains stuff when he give it to us; the other teacher just give it to us and expect us to know how to do it.
I: What does the first teacher do to help you get it?
S: Like when he give us new math, like yesterday, he gives a example on the board, and if I don't understand when I do it on my own, you tell him and then he say "all right" and come help you.
I: When do you have the most trouble learning?
S: Language arts and science.
I: Why?
S: What I said earlier. The teacher just put it on the board and if you don't know how, the teacher get angry. I try to get help but when I come after school, they gotta go somewhere and can't help you . . . like when I ask somebody to help me, just because some other kid won't need help, then they think others won't either; some kids are smarter.
I: If you got more help, could you get a better grade?
S: Mmhmm. (251611)

S: In one class, my teacher has a bad attitude. He takes out his anger on you. He barely teaches. All we do is read books. If we don't know something, all he says is just "figure it out yourself." In my other class, we learn how to do letters. She wants to teach us what we don't know. If you raise your hand, she will explain it to us and show us how to do it. Some teachers just teach more.
I: But in your other class?
S: He just has us read books. He tells us he has his education. If we don't like it, don't come to class. My mom didn't send me here just to read books. (327612)

I: Do you learn more in some classes?
S: Yeah.
I: Which ones?

S: In social studies we do the work, pay attention, and don't get out of our seat.

I: Why?

S: The teacher helps you out a lot. Other teachers just write things on the board and don't explain it. (407621)

Students argued that creating a more supportive atmosphere would have positive effects on discipline.

I: Do students act up in your class?

S: Most of them, they don't have enough stuff to stay in.

I: What do you mean?

S: They don't try. They don't think they can do it.

I: Do you have some advice?

S: Have like a family group, small groups, to talk about problems, and teachers could give some advice.

I: Do you do that now?

S: No.

I: Why do you think that would work?

S: They would build like . . . make some feel like they are cared about. (260612)

Thus, students encountered a range of situations in which conditions festered to the point that they learned little. Their depictions changed each year in terms of which classes were involved, but not in terms of frequency. Each year, each day, students alternately walked into classrooms where they learned and where they did not.

A NEED TO SCALE UP WITHIN SCHOOLS

The preceding discussion suggests that little actually changed during the students' three years in middle school. Significant change, of course, takes time, and it may be that the effects of what the District had done to date would be realized down the road. Also, it may have been that students were simply poor informants about change; after all they had little basis for comparison. Thus, the above discussion should not be considered an unabashed indictment of the District's accomplishments over the time period.

Nevertheless, in the students' descriptions of what they knew best— the classroom, there lay an unavoidable message. Within and across schools, students had dissimilar experiences from one classroom to the next and had unequal access to teaching that led to learning. It is improbable that any claim of reform progress would have either credibility or staying power until it demonstrated that the quality of education in one classroom and in one school was essentially the same as in another classroom or school, and that the level of quality was steadily improving.

Educational reform observers have noted the necessity of "scaling up" a reform to a critical mass of schools within a district in order to have a substantial impact on the achievement of many children (Bodilly, 1998; Elmore, 1996). Our students described the necessity of going to scale "within" a school in order to have a consistent and reinforcing influence on what and how much students learned.

The one conclusion that seems reasonable to draw from this is that Children Achieving had not yet thoroughly and consistently penetrated the day-to-day lives of students. This criticism should not be uniquely applied to Children Achieving. It is a constant companion of reform throughout the United States. But "pockets of success" do not breed "success for all"; and "success for some" only entrenches the historically inequitable distribution of high quality educational experiences for urban youth.

The next chapter portrays in detail the nature of these differences and their effects on students.

THREE

PEDAGOGICAL, CONTENT, AND CLASSROOM ENVIRONMENT DIFFERENCES WITHIN AND ACROSS FIVE SCHOOLS

The students' comments about themselves, their schools, and their teachers touched on aspects of their education that should have been sensitive to a reform intended to affect the core processes of schooling. Or at least we assumed that the District intended that the road from its ten goals to improved student achievement would pass through the classroom. We hoped that students' indications of little change in this respect mostly reflected the relative newness of the Philadelphia School District's agenda, but feared that the available resources were too thinly spread to have much impact.

One persistent thread running through the students' descriptions seemed to us to be particularly worthy of immediate consideration because it pointed to a potentially devastating obstacle to reform progress— the dramatic instructional differences from one classroom to the next. Students' depictions of these differences suggested that there was an embedded and endemic unevenness to the schools' instructional programs. Children Achieving would eventually have to smooth this situation out if the District was planning to tout test score improvement as a function of higher quality instruction for all students.

We saw at least three types of classroom differences in the interviews that influenced what and how much students learned. One type was pedagogical. Not surprisingly, students said that various teachers relied on different means of instruction. Despite the overwhelming persuasiveness of the literature on learning styles and multiple intelligences, there were teachers who opted to rely on instructional strategies that were primarily suited to one style or intelligence rather than to several. Students, of course, did not refer to research on learning to compare their teachers; they only knew that some classes frustrated them and others did not.

A second type of instructional difference was with the **content** of the class. The District had a guide, commonly called the Frameworks, that identified topics to be covered in each subject at each grade level. Still, teachers apparently found it difficult to cover all the topics designated as appropriate for their students in a school year. Thus, they had to pick and choose what to emphasize in day-to-day lessons. Therefore, students in one class ended the year expert in certain areas while students in the same grade but having a different teacher developed skills and knowledge in another aspect of the same subject.

The third type of difference was less subtle. Students juxtaposed classrooms in which learning took place and those where minimal learning occurred. These **classroom environment** differences had little to do with gradations of individuals' acquisition of knowledge or with nuances in the content covered; instead, environmental characteristics determined whether the majority of students learned anything at all. Either because a teacher was reluctant to go back over previously introduced material or did not appear to be very willing to offer extra help or did little to engage the students in learning, students in each school were able to describe situations in which little learning took place at any point in the year.

This section looks at each of these instructional differences in turn. We want to emphasize that all three were pervasive. Every one of the students in the study reported on pedagogical differences, although not necessarily with complaint. Although individual students were rarely in a situation that enabled them to comment on content differences within the same subject in a school, they collectively did so in each of the five schools. And, nearly every student, unfortunately, had firsthand experience with the debilitating influence of classroom environment differences during their three-year sojourn in middle school.

PEDAGOGICAL DIFFERENCES — THE CASE OF SCIENCE

Rightly or wrongly, the folklore of teaching argues that some subjects are more suited to certain instructional strategies than others. For example, "math has to be taught sequentially" or "social studies is the place for classroom discussions." The national associations of teachers who specialize in each subject area have all embarked on efforts to remove the folklore from the fact with respect to best practice. We do not wish to enter that arena, and we are not in a position to support or dispute Philadelphia's teachers' agreement with the emerging standards of best practice. Still, it seemed advisable to examine students' comments about pedagogy only within a subject area rather than across them, just in case some of their teachers still held to these long-standing beliefs about teaching their respective subjects.

In each of the five buildings, students who took a particular subject from one teacher described an entirely different approach to teaching from students who had another teacher for the same subject. Nowhere was this difference more noticeable than in science classes.

Current science standards emphasize student problem-solving abilities, which include formulating problems and designing investigations to shed light on possible answers (see Allen & Lederman, 1998; Windschitl, 1999). This inquiry-centered approach emphasizes "hands-on, minds-on" activities that enable students to test predictions. Students in each school described great variation in how often they were able to engage in hands-on activities. Some students had few opportunities to do them and described instruction where the focus was on learning important facts. Others did experiments and projects, but all the procedures and steps were clearly spelled out. There were only a few cases where students were challenged to think about underlying principles and construct experiments that would allow them to test alternative explanations.

Characteristic of a traditional approach to teaching science were working from the textbook and taking notes. Descriptions such as the following were frequent:

I: What do you do in science?
S: Mostly we work out of the text.
I: What kinds of things are you studying?
S: We are studying earthquakes and volcanoes.
I: What kinds of things do you do with the textbook?
S: We do vocabulary. We read the chapter and get the vocabulary words. After each section in the book, we do a section review.
I: Do you do experiments?
S: No, but sometimes we do reports. (101631)

S: We read in the textbook and then we take notes. We also answer questions from the "check and explain" part of the book.

I: Do you do experiments?
S: Not that often. We did a couple this year. (300611)

Occasionally students would report that they did "hands-on" activities in science. The phrase, however, encompassed a wide range of tasks. In essence, "hands-on" referred to anything the students did beyond listening to the teacher, copying notes from the board, or answering specific questions from the textbook.

S: We have been doing projects on the planets. We need to get the facts and draw a picture.
I: Where do you go to get your facts?
S: I go to the library and copy things out of a book. (136612)

S: We do lots of projects.
I: Can you give me an example?
S: Yeah, I did a project on acid rain.
I: What did you do?
S: I did some research and wrote a report. (312611)

S: We had to do science fair projects, even if we didn't enter the science fair.
I: How did you know what to do?
S: [The teacher] just gave us lists of what we needed to do. (522611)

It was the rare exception when students described doing open-ended activities where they decided what they would do and how they would go about it:

S: We do a lot of group projects.
I: How often do you do these?
S: Two or three a month.
I: What kinds of things are you doing?
S: We just did a model on the phases of the moon.
I: Did your teacher tell you what to do?
S: No, we had to figure out our roles by ourselves. (329612)

S: We are doing a garden project [in the school courtyard]. We had to figure out what we were going to plant, and we had to describe the plants [we wanted to plant]. We also do experiments that we make up on our own. (332612)

These different approaches to teaching science appeared simultaneously in the same school in the same grade. For example, in School #2, one teacher relied heavily on the textbook, copying notes, and completing chapter reviews (Teacher #2-A), whereas that teacher's grade-level colleague concentrated on hands-on activities and experiments (Teacher #2-B).

I: What do you do in science class?

S: We know we have to write. Teacher #2-A always has three boards of stuff. Teacher #2-A be writing with us. It often takes the whole period.

I: Do you do anything else?

S: Sometimes we read. Sometimes we do worksheets or projects. (209611)

S: We get three to five minutes to get ready. Then we copy notes from the board. Next we open the text and discuss what we have been reading and what notes we have taken.

I: How long do you spend doing each of these?

S: About twenty to twenty-five minutes writing notes and fifteen to twenty minutes discussing. (211611)

S: Most of the time we write notes from the board. We usually have three blackboards of notes. It takes about thirty minutes. After thirty minutes, Teacher #2-A starts going over it. He goes to the textbook and shows us his way and the book way.

I: Do you do experiments?

S: Yeah, but we haven't done any for a long time—since March or April [interviewed in June].

I: What else do you do?

S: We do lots of tests, most every Friday. He prefers long answers to his questions. (225611)

In contrast, students from another class down the hall described their experience as primarily being hands-on experiments and projects, with the textbook serving as a secondary resource:

I: What do you do in science class?

S: We mostly do science projects.

I: How often?

S: A lot!

I: Can you remember some examples?

S: We did rocket engines, we wrote about the greenhouse effect, and we tested how many drops of water fit on a coin.

I: Do you use your textbook much?

S: Not as much as we do projects. (205612)

S: All we do is experiments and projects. We study procedure and hypothesis.

I: Do you use your textbook much?

S: Not really. It's just in our book bag most of the time. Sometimes we do homework in it. (207612)

S: We mostly do projects.

I: Can you give me an example?

S: I just finished a science fair poster on hard and soft water. Also, at the beginning of the year we did reports on black scientists.

I: How did you know who to do a report on?

S: Teacher #2-B gave us a list and we got to pick from the list.

I: Do you use the textbook much?

S: No, not much. We usually just talk about what's in the textbook.

I: Is that helpful?

S: I like it better than just reading and taking notes. (223611)

Varied science experiences similar to those in School #2 were prevalent in the other schools as well. For example, all the students in School #1 reported spending a good deal of time reading from the text and copying notes from the board. However, some claimed that this was almost all that they did in class and others noted that they did a variety of projects and experiments.

S: We outline the chapter.

I: Who creates the outline?

S: The teacher do it and we copy it. Sometimes we do it on our own.

I: What else do you do?

S: We answer questions from the end of the chapter.

I: Do you do experiments?

S: No, not many. We did some at the beginning of the year. (105612)

I: What are you doing in science?

S: We are working on fossils and we are also studying weather maps. That's fun cause we get to act like we are weather reporters and the teacher videotaped us.

I: Do you do experiments?

S: Yeah. We're working on one now with fossils.

I: How about projects?

S: We have been doing some weather forecasting. (111611)

In School #5, all but two students talked about being preoccupied with doing their science fair projects (we were in the school just before they were due). Most students said they had been working on them for two or three months. When they were not working on science fair projects, students reported spending almost all their time reading from the text, copying notes, and answering questions. There was little or no mention of experiments, apart from the science fair in this particular building.

I: What have you been doing in science?

S: We have been learning about the stars and the planets.

I: How do you learn about that?

S: We read about it in the textbook and the teacher explains it. We do worksheets and then we do the section review in the book.

I: Do you do many experiments?

S: No, just about two. But we did just finish our science fair projects. Everyone had to do one. (501612)

An understandable initial reaction to the above descriptions might be, "So? Teachers have always had the freedom to decide how they should teach." The students might have answered, "But how a teacher teaches affects how and what we learn."

They made this point clearly back in the first year of the study. The students could not have been expected to be familiar with the constructivist literature nor the names of Dewey, Piaget, and Vygotsky. Nevertheless, they constructed a compelling case for being active as a valuable means to making school-related learning more attractive to them. As students talked about the kinds of work that helped them learn best and what teachers could do to make learning more interesting, they repeatedly stated: "give us projects," "make it fun," and "let us work with other students." Two-thirds of our overall sample in the first year (248 out of

361) mentioned either these phrases or related preferences for class-room activities such as "use my imagination," "find information and do research," "make things," and "play games that help us learn." In fact, mentions of these active learning-related ideas cropped up 464 times in the interviews, nearly two mentions per student.

Doing projects and experiments were the activities most frequently mentioned in response to questions about what kind of work students liked doing best or that helped them learn the best, receiving 133 of the 464 references to activities. The sheer number of students who discussed these activities was impressive; the "whys" were even more so because they revealed an enthusiasm for doing work of this type. Students claimed that if work was fun, they learned better.

> It's fun and I can learn. (166611)

> It's fun experimenting with things; when you do it, you get something out of it. (550612)

> Because you can have fun and learn at the same time; it teaches you more about the subject. You know how they say if you learn, you explore and then you be successful. (450611)

They also argued that the activities required them to think, to use their imaginations. In some instances, what they had to think about in school corresponded to things they were curious about generally.

> You get to think about what you do. (269611)

> 'Cause some of them [projects] is like you can imagine what you want to do and I do all kinds of stuff, like making a one-leg dog, putting materials together. (358612)

> You get to experiment with things, hands-on type things, stuff you be wondering about. (282812)

We should point out that the students reinforced the research on learning styles. Not every student expressed a wish that teachers would allow them to do projects and experiments. As one of these contrarians countered, "I like doing worksheets; I don't like doing all that research." (170611) Still, an overwhelming number of them explained that they learned best when they were active; and as the pedagogical differences

Kinesthetic learners/naturalist spatial

described above illustrate, an overwhelming number of students certainly did not find themselves in such situations in science.

Content Differences — The Case of English

Just as there are standards about quality science instruction, in English the emphasis on understanding the writing process is a key element of what students are expected to know and be able to do. In addition to being exposed to different kinds of writing activities, our students encountered divergent definitions of what it meant to be a good writer. Some students claimed their teachers had no rules for writing. Others said their teachers focused on details like punctuation, capitalization, and indentation. Still others described teachers who used process definitions of good writing, referring to beginnings, middles, and conclusions and/or getting across the main point with supporting examples.

Some of the students apparently had not internalized any particular rules for producing a quality piece of writing. Instead, they relied on the teacher's judgment, in the absence of which students had no conception of whether they had done well or poorly.

I: Do you do much writing in your English class?

S: No, we don't do that much.

I: How do you know if you have written a quality piece of work when you are writing?

S: The teacher just looks it over, and she says it's "good." (102612)

I: Are there any special steps you need to follow when writing a good essay?

S: No, not really. Sometimes the teacher might give us a story to get us started. We just need to listen to the teacher's instructions, jot down notes, and go home and study. (303611)

I: Do you know what it takes to write a good essay?

S: No, she [teacher] don't tell us. (401621)

Other students suggested that the quality of what they wrote derived from using proper punctuation or grammar:

I: What does it take to write a good essay?

S: If I do what she taught me. You know, it has to have good grammar, the sentences have to be right—complex ones are better, the punctuation has to be good, and the sentences have to make sense. You can't have no sentence fragments or run-ons. (104612)

I: How do you know if you have written a good essay in language arts?
S: If it's neat, has no mistakes, and has what she wants. (226612)

I: How often do you write?
S: Everyday!
I: What kinds of things do you write.
S: Notes off the board.
I: When you write your own sentences, are there any special steps you follow to make sure it is good quality?
S: Yeah, we have the steps on the wall. You have to capitalize, make sure you have periods, punctuation must be right, and you have to write neatly. (309611)

Yet others, when they spoke of writing, focused more on a process that involved revision and refinement.

I: Do you have any guidelines for writing?
S: Yes. First, you need to think about it. Then you need to write a rough draft. After that you need to proof it. Finally you do a regular draft.
I: Does you teacher ever have you redo a regular draft?
S: Yes, He'll hand it back and have us redo it.
I: Do you prefer that?
S: Yes. They can make sure I do it right. If they know I can do better, I want someone who will push me. (327612)

S: You have to write the right stuff.
I: How do you know if you have the right stuff?
S: You have to write lots and you have to correct it after you do the first draft.
I: Who helps you with the revisions?
S: The students do sometimes, but mostly the teacher. (125611)

I: Are there steps you follow in preparing a good essay?
S: Yes. You need to first make a rough draft. Then you need to
    revise it. Next you need to write a final draft. And then you
    have to publish it.
I: Do you do much writing?
S: Yes, a lot. Mostly everyday. (310611)

As with science, the five schools had contrasting writing emphases
within their walls. By way of example, students at School #3 encountered
a large number of different English teachers. "Writing," in the students'
minds, encompassed maintaining a journal every day, constructing a
portfolio, doing creative and narrative writing, filling in the blanks on a
handout, doing worksheets, and answering questions from the book.
Only a handful of students made any mention of the writing process, with
one of them only vaguely remembering that "there were steps on the
wall."

I: What about writing in English class?
S: We have paragraphs with blank spaces and we have to write
    in the missing words. We also have to answer questions and
    write paragraphs.
I: Do you write essays or journal entries?
S: No, not in English. Only in social studies. (332612)

I: How often do you write in English class?
S: Every day.
I: What kind of writing do you do?
S: Mostly just answering questions from the textbook.
I: Are there any special steps you follow when you are writ-
    ing?
S: No, just as long as you know what you're doing, [you'll get
    a good grade]. (322612)

I: How often are you writing in English class?
S: Every day. We write in our journal.
I: What kinds of things do you write about?
S: If I could pick my high school of choice, what would it be
    and why? We are also collecting all of our narrative essays
    into a writing portfolio. We are attaching a cover sheet to
    each sample explaining why we chose it and what we
    learned from it. (300611)

For the students at School #4 writing included taking notes and doing worksheets. There was an occasional reference to writing essays, and about one-third of the students talked about writing in journals. Several students also mentioned a current writing project in which they were working on career activities, such as employment applications, resumes, and letters of employment.

S: In English we are mostly working on projects.
I: What project are you working on now?
S: We are learning how to do a work application—filling out forms, getting letters and references from our family.
I: Do you do much writing in this class?
S: Mostly vocabulary words—writing sentences and definitions.
I: Do you do many essays?
S: No, not much. (401621)

S: We do a lot of things from the textbook or from the newspaper. We do questions from the newspaper and write a paragraph.
I: What does it take to write a good paragraph?
S: It has to have eight lines, the right words need to be capitalized, and no misspelled words.
I: Does your teacher have you redo poorly written paragraphs?
S: Only if we have misspelled words. (414622)

As a final example, most of the students at School #5 reported that writing involved copying notes, answering questions, writing sentences, or doing spelling words. Only a quarter of the students mentioned either writing poetry or creating their own stories/essays.

I: How often do you write in English class?
S: Every day.
I: What kinds of things are you writing?
S: We copy notes from the board and we do dictionary work. We also answer questions from our workbook.
I: Do you ever write your own stories?
S: No. (503612)

I: How about writing?

S: We do that more than reading. We do lots of that for homework, especially unpunctuated sentences. We mostly learn stuff from elementary school—like punctuation.

I: Do you write anything else?

S: Sometimes we will write short stories. (505611)

I: How often are you writing in your English class?

S: Every day.

I: What kinds of things are you writing?

S: We answer questions from the book and we take notes. Maybe once or twice a month we will write our own stories or essays.

I: What does it take to get an A on a writing assignment?

S: You need to get punctuation right. You can't have any grammatical errors. You also need to know how to explain it. You have to have it in the right order. (522611)

There was no doubt that teachers in all five buildings were putting an emphasis on student writing. However, what it meant to write well in the context of individual classrooms varied tremendously. Thus, while most students were learning to write, they were often learning something entirely different from peers within and across the five buildings.

Classroom Environment Differences — Two Examples

In chapter 2, we described in detail classrooms in which there were "cracks in the classroom floor" caused either by a revolving door of substitute teachers, disruptive students who forced teachers to deal with behavior at the expense of instruction, or support scarce classrooms where students did not get repeated explanations or extra help. We heard similar stories each year, and, in the final year, the examples seemed to be as prevalent among regular teachers as interim ones, underscoring the fact that Children Achieving's efforts were not yet noticeable to students.

From the students' perspective, some classrooms' environments were such that little learning, if any, took place. Whereas pedagogical differences affected who learned—based on the match between how a teacher taught and how students learned best—and content differences influenced what students learned, these environmental differences were associated with no students (at least among the ones we interviewed from the classes) reporting that their time in class had been well spent. Interestingly, the same students could describe neighboring classrooms where teachers fostered markedly productive learning environments.

We offer two examples. In both, we rely on students to compare two of their teachers, to assess the amount of learning that went on in each classroom, and to explain the differences.

The reader should keep in mind that the two examples are not the most dramatic we could have selected. The dramatic cases generally came from comparisons of "out of control" classrooms and orderly ones. These environments certainly merit attention. They were all too common, according to the students, and to many other accounts of inner-city schools (Ross, 1999). They also were obvious to most residents in the buildings. The problem was not so much identifying learning-bereft classrooms as it was finding teachers skilled in working in urban situations who planned to remain in the position for a while.

The following examples were more subtle in that instruction itself rather than classroom management seemed to lie at the root of contrasting classroom dynamics, at least according to the students who experienced both situations. Students connected how the teacher conducted the class, the students' relationship with the teacher, and the students' sense of whether they were learning anything as the ingredients for creating a productive classroom.

School #1: Two Teachers on the Same Team

In School #1, the students had two teachers for their core academic subjects who worked together as a team. Typically, one handled math and science while the second taught social studies and language arts, with both sharing the same group of students.

One such group of students saw their social studies/language arts teacher (#1-A) as someone they could learn from and relate to well, while they seemed to constantly do battle with their math and science teacher (#1-B). Students portrayed #1-B as overdemanding, impatient, and insensitive; #1-A seemed to be just the opposite.

> I: Have you had a good year?
> S: Teacher #1-B has an attitude problem. She wants us to be so good the first time. She wants us to always be perfect. She has us walk in a line in the hallway. We are the only class in the school to do that.

I: Why do you think she has you do that?

S: She wants to impress the principal.

I: Is there anything else she does that bothers you?

S: She is the only one [teacher](who won't go over things. She never comes in with a smile; she is always evil. By not going over it, we got a bad attitude. I haven't learned nothing in her class. Only three students have, but they were ones who were held back and they all have tutors.

I: Do you mostly cover new material in the class or is it review?

S: Some of it's new. Actually, we do more new stuff as the year goes along. But we stay on something new for only one day. The teacher never goes back over it. All we do is have tests on it.

I: What do you do in math class [with this teacher]?

S: The teacher teach real fast. The teacher talks fast. If we ask her to say it over, she has an attitude. The teacher takes out home problems on us.

I: What do you do after the teacher teaches new work?

S: Then we do our homework. But the teacher don't check it. We could cheat and she would never know!

I: How about Teacher #1-A.

S: If we don't get it, he will go over it. That teacher is nice.

I: Do students come in after school for help?

S: Yeah!

I: How many?

S: A lot. We come in for help on Monday and Thursday.

I: How about help from Teacher #1-B?

S: That teacher helps us on Monday and Wednesday, but she always has too much to do. We just sit there and read a book.

I: Tell me more about Teacher #1-A?

S: One boy in the class, he do all his work now. If it wasn't for Teacher #1-A, he wouldn't do nothing. At the beginning of the year, he don't do nothing; now he does. He wouldn't even take the SAT-9s; all he did was just bubbled in the answers.

I: Why do you think that student is working now?

S: Cause Teacher #1-A took time out to help him and talk to him.

I: How else are your two teachers different?

S: Teacher #1-B puts us down. Teacher #1-A say to us, don't drop out. Teacher #1-B starts us with an F and expect us to bring it up. Teacher #1-A starts us with an A. He also has us stay after school until we turn the work in. If we do a bad test, we can retake it 'til we get a good grade. With Teacher #1-B, we don't have retakes. (106612)

The students zeroed in on how the two teachers handled work that was not turned in on time as indicative of their respective approaches to students.

I: How do your teachers deal with work that you don't turn in?

S: Teacher #1-A tells me what is late. Whatever we miss, Teacher #1-B just has us sit in our seats after school and checks on us. Teacher #1-A is more willing to help.

I: What does Teacher #1-A do to make the work more understandable?

S: He puts some of our reading books on tape. And one time we went to 33rd and Sansom where we got to act out a play we were studying [Othello]. We also looked at movies and saw how the characters act out the parts.

I: How about Teacher #1-B?

S: At times, she just say, "Don't bother me; I've told you once. Ask your classmates for help." She says to call your "study buddy." She don't like to help or care for some people. She only cares about nice, quiet people who do all their work. (127612)

Perhaps the most significant difference between the two teachers was how they handled students who needed additional help. As noted in chapter 4, the willingness of a teacher to work with students until they understood a concept was a highly valued trait. One of the teachers on this team promoted independence and self-reliance by encouraging students to figure things out for themselves, while the other offered a support net to students until they could do the work on their own.

I: Do you feel like you are prepared for high school?

S: No, I ain't that good in math, but I'm ready in the rest of them.

I: Why are you doing so poorly in math [student admitted she was failing]?

S: It's the way the teacher teaches. She just gives it to us and don't explain it. She expect us to know it. The kids put their hands up and she says, "Put your hand down, you should know it." I haven't seen one report card with an A or B on it. She just has us do problems from the book. The teacher calls us up individually and checks 'em. She just marks 'em wrong and puts your grade in the book.

I: But what if you don't understand? What does the teacher do?

S: She says to keep trying and gets an attitude. She starts yelling so everyone just ignores her. They [the students] go on strike.

I: What happens when you refuse to do the work?

S: She gives us a detention and call our parents in. Then she starts bringing up things from the beginning of the year and we just ignore it.

I: How about Teacher #1-A?

S: We learn a lot.

I: What does Teacher #1-A do that helps you learn?

S: He brings us movies, and we act things out most every day. He makes it fun and don't get an attitude every five minutes. Sometimes we discuss things for a whole hour or so. We also read interesting stuff.

I: Like what?

S: Maya Angelou.

I: Why is that interesting?

S: We read about people fighting, a girl who was raped, things that happen in real life. He tells us how not to act as a young lady.

I: What happens if you don't understand your work with Teacher #1-A?

S: He calls us to the desk and spends about fifteen minutes with us. If the whole group can't get it, he will stop the class and explain. He gives us steps to do it. (129612)

Another student underlined the value students placed on a teacher's taking time to explain their work and making sure that everyone understood what they were supposed to do:

I: Are you getting a good education this year?

S: Not really.

I: Why not?

S: My teacher (Teacher #1-B) just teaches a lesson once. If you ask for help, she gets an attitude. She says "I already taught it once, I'm not going to teach it again; you weren't paying attention." She just teaches too fast and don't take the time to teach it right.

I: Why?

S: She only wants to teach it once.

I: What about Teacher #1-A?

S: He takes time and teaches. If you don't understand, he takes time to explain.

I: Can you give me an example?

S: In social studies we were doing slave trade. The test we did was different than what we learned [and we didn't get good grades on it].

I: What did the teacher do?

S: He explained it again and wrote notes for us. I took a retest and went from a D to a C.

I: What else does Teacher #1-A do?

S: He talks to you about it. He makes sure you understand and know what you are doing.

I: How does he do that?

S: He checks everybody's work and explains it if it is not right.

I: Does he do that often?

S: Yes. He do it every day. (136612)

*School #4: A Comparison between Students' Initial
Teacher and a Replacement*

One of the problems that these students faced was a revolving door of teachers, and rarely did they view a replacement teacher as an improvement over the initial one. However, in an exception to this rule, the following School #4 students said that they had learned almost nothing with their original teacher, while they were very excited about the replacement. Students did not mince words in portraying how they felt about this.

I: Are you learning a lot this year?

S: Not in the beginning. Teacher #4-A [a science teacher] just wrote notes on the board. I didn't learn nothing. Now we have Teacher #4-B and we do projects. We have fun. We are learning lots.

I: What happened to the first teacher?

S: I'm not sure, I heard he got fired. (418622)

I: Have you had a good year?

S: Yeah, I'm learning a lot.

I: How do you know?

S: The teachers give us a lot of work, but I had trouble with one teacher [Teacher #4-A], all he did was wrote on the board and told us to copy it. He never taught us anything.

I: What happened to Teacher #4-A?

S: His blood pressure went up.

I: How about Teacher #4-B? How is that teacher different?

S: She tells us what's in the book, has us do questions, and helps us when we get stuck. The first thing she said when she arrived in the class was "Raise your hand, if you need help." (428621)

The students' faces even changed when they talked about the two teachers, a scrunched frown followed by a relaxed smile. Their descriptions sounded almost rehearsed in their repetition.

All the first teacher did was write on the board and make us copy. Now my favorite teacher is Teacher #4-B. That teacher can do more things with us, like experiments. We did starfish, looked through a microscope, cut open a pig's eye, and the teacher already ordered the frogs. (466621)

The old teacher only do 15 problems on the board. We copy everything on the board. The new teacher bring in research specimen. (464611)

Everybody like the new teacher. The old teacher never did experiments. The new teacher don't yell, [she] just look at you and everybody be quiet. Everybody be quiet 'cause they wanna do it. She brought in mice, a snake, a pig. (467612)

I know nothing about science. I never learned anything. The old teacher put questions and answers on the board. That is not the correct way to teach. The new teacher is more interesting and captures my attention, talks about interesting stuff. (453622)

The old teacher would just put questions on the board and we would read a book and get the answers. Now we got a new teacher. She explains things to us. We starting to digest [sic] starfish. That is more interesting. (461622)

The District's accountability system would not have been sensitive enough to detect the differences in the two teachers' instructional environments. However, the students' testimonies served well:

It's the only class with homework, and we pay attention and do good. When the test come, we know what we doing so we get a good grade. (466621)

I learn better with the experiment cause we really learn stuff. Copying from the board is doing what somebody else already did. (464611)

When the old teacher gave me a grade, I was like, "I hardly deserve this 'cause he didn't teach nothing." I did all the work, but I didn't understand it. (461622)

As we began to encounter students who were describing this science class, we felt that their accounts represented a distinct departure from the kinds of debilitating classroom environments students had complained about in previous years. We were used to students talking about "out of control" classrooms in which the residents did daily battle with one another. This situation was different. The initial science teacher simply had not created an atmosphere that enabled the students to learn or that encouraged them to want to learn. The atmosphere was more emotionally benign than the usual examples, but the consequence was the same—wasted time in a subject. We found that these more subtle situations also affected significant numbers of students, perhaps in the same way as the more dramatic cases, but unfortunately less visible and/or less obviously requiring immediate correction.

Isn't this pedagogical?
or at least both - attitude of T
+ pedagogy

STUDENTS FOCUSED ON INSTRUCTIONAL,
RATHER THAN PERSONAL, STYLE

Some teachers in the participating schools worried that students would talk badly about them because they thought students did not necessarily like them. However, students seemed to dissociate a teacher's personal style from his or her instructional style, perhaps better than many adults did. Personal style affected how likable a teacher was; instructional style determined how effective the teacher was. Personal style derived from whether a teacher was funny or stern, animated or expressionless, dynamic or passive. Instructional style sprung from understandings about how humans learn.

Students talked favorably about teachers because of how they taught. Thus, we cannot dismiss the differences they described among the teachers as simply differences in teacher "style" because their focus was on instructional rather than personal style; and instructional style, they cautioned, had a significant impact on who learned, what they learned, and how much they learned.

This book could end here, a pronouncement of uneven education. It would then join the litany of similar assessments of reform. But this noted lack of progress is actually only a beginning point. Educational reform in Philadelphia had an untapped ally—the students. While one only had to walk around the schools briefly to sense the uneasy and fragile relationships between young people and adults, the potential for an alliance was there. The students in these five middle schools knew what kind of teachers they wanted. They wanted teachers who "stayed on students" to complete assignments, went out of their way to provide help, explained things until the "light bulb went on" for the whole class, varied classroom activities, controlled student behavior without ignoring the lesson, and understood students' situations and factored that into their lessons. Children Achieving would have been hard-pressed to disavow these characteristics as worthy products of professional development. Chapter 4 elaborates what students meant by these qualities.

FOUR

THE TEACHERS STUDENTS WANTED

The students in our study were among the lowest performing in the city. More of them read below grade level, performed poorly on basic mathematics, and wrote in an unskilled way than did their middle grades counterparts around the city, much less in the suburbs. This specific performance gap on tests is but a mirror of a national trend in which children of poverty score significantly lower on various standardized tests than children of wealth. Numerous explanations for this gap abound, most of which correctly identify that this educational dilemma has deep societal roots.

However, while society changes glacially, children continue to move through their schooling years at a much quicker and unrelenting pace. Our students did not have the luxury of waiting for tomorrow's solutions. That is why educational reformers must look inward, within schools, for strategies that benefit current cohorts of students. Recent thinking by Jencks and Phillips (1998) underscores this necessity. They argue convincingly that the performance gap can be reduced by paying much closer attention to the nature of students' classroom experiences. Dwelling on matters of heredity and background, they claim, is unproductive and, in fact, simply wrong.

Jencks and Phillips are not too far behind Philadelphia's middle school students' thinking in this regard. For the last three years, the students filled our interviews with descriptions of teachers who helped and hindered their learning. These descriptions were consistent and compelling—and succinct about the kinds of teachers they felt would best prepare them for the futures they desired. Indeed, the students were absolutely positive that they and their peers could succeed well in certain classroom environments.

Students did not want teachers to find excuses to not teach them, to leave a student alone just because the student chose not to participate, or to let students decide on their own to work or not. They did not want teachers to give in to disruptions to the exclusion of instruction. They did not want teachers who failed to find the time to provide extra help. They did not want teachers to quit explaining something to someone just because the task or problem had already been explained several times before. They did not want teachers who ignored students' problems or who taught content devoid of meaning in students' daily lives. They did not want teachers who expected little of them.

Instead, students wanted to be in classrooms where:

- The teacher "stayed on students" to complete assignments.
- The teacher was able to control student behavior without ignoring the lesson.
- The teacher went out of his or her way to provide help.
- The teacher explained things until the "light bulb went on" for the whole class.
- The teacher provided students with a variety of activities through which to learn.
- The teacher understood students' situations and factored that into their lessons.

When we say "students wanted" these qualities present in their classrooms, we mean that the overwhelming majority of students reiterated these characteristics at every opportunity in the interviews over the three-year period. These are not "the survey says" kinds of answers. Offering the percentage of students who responded with these "wants" is not very meaningful because the number of dissenters would be in the single digits—in absolute numbers not percentages.

More important than the discrete elements in the list of desired qualities above is the sense that students were pointing to a more encompassing holistic principle to which they wanted teachers to adhere. Essentially we interpreted students to be saying that the effective teachers adhered to a **"no excuses"** policy. That is, there were no acceptable reasons why every student eventually could not complete his or her work, and there were no acceptable reasons why a teacher would "give up" on a child. The premise was that every child should complete every assignment and that it was the teacher's job to ensure that this happened. Accepting this premise meant that the teacher would have to use a host of strategies, including the six listed above. But the particular strategies used were less important than the underlying belief they symbolized: that every child had to have the in-school support necessary for learning to occur.

For example, one student told us about several ways his teachers had helped him make it through eighth grade. This was no small task. As a seventh grader, he said he was "suspended every week" but that it had happened only a "few" times in the eighth grade. He perceived that he had turned around his school performance and this was directly attributable to teachers' interventions. These included: giving him extra help—especially in the school's after-hours tutoring program, being "stricter" with his work completion and behavior, giving him "high school" assignments, talking about subject matter rather than just using the textbook, and reinforcing the importance of getting an education for his future life. He was greatly appreciative of their efforts. He also recognized the common thread that ran through the teachers' actions, concluding:

The whole point of it is to keep you from failing. (508611)

The strategies then were the tools the teacher used to construct a safety net, and these tools had utility only if they were effective for that purpose. The implication was that teachers could not take solace in having implemented "effective practices" in situations in which students did not respond. Instead, the onus was on the teacher to devise alternative means of reaching out to those students.

Shouldering the responsibility for learning was understandably difficult for teachers and an admittedly unfair burden for them to bear alone. However, the cracks in these urban classroom floors were wide. Poverty, meager educational resources, crime, and all the attendant problems in the students' neighborhoods conspired to fling open the gates to failure. There was no recourse for schools but to attempt to compensate for this societal lack of support from within. Some teachers in every one of the five schools created classrooms in which this support could be found. Students recognized and valued this; and then wondered why every classroom could not be that way.

This chapter lays out six qualities that students wanted their teachers to have, qualities that they believed would better enable them to learn and be successful in school. We caution against thinking of these as a simple checklist (although PEF did turn them into the content for a poster it inserted in each copy of the third-year report.) While it was true that teachers using more of these were more valued by students, the real purpose of these qualities was to create a noticeable support net underneath student performance.

The first part of this chapter revisits two of the teachers described in chapter 3 and adds a description of a third to illustrate what an implemented "no excuses" teaching approach sounded like in students' voices. The second part of the chapter examines each of the six qualities in turn to provide a more in-depth sense of what students meant by the terms.

THREE TEACHERS STUDENTS PRAISED

Teacher #1-A taught both English and Social Studies. Whenever we entered the class to get students for interviews, it appeared that students were working—at least there was not the boisterous outburst of comments and off-task behavior that accompanied our appearance in other classrooms. In students' comments presented earlier, Teacher #1-A relied on a variety of means by which he cajoled, nudged, and commanded the students to complete their assignments. These included his taking a keen interest even in the unmotivated students, always providing words of encouragement, giving students the opportunity to make up work, inviting students to come in for after-school tutoring, going over work until everyone understood it, making the work relevant to students' lives, and engaging students in the work with hands-on activities.

Individually, any one of these efforts might have spurred one or two or several students to put forth more effort than they might otherwise have. Collectively, the strategies spurred nearly all, if not everyone, to finish their work. The effect was not unnoticed. Students found themselves behaving better in the class than they did in others, appreciating the teacher's willingness to help them understand the work, and achieving the best grades they could.

> I: Do you behave better for some teachers than others?
> S: With Teacher #1-A, everybody cool. In my other class, people are more talking.
> I: Why is that?
> S: He have more respect for us.
> I: What do you mean?
> S: If you have questions you don't understand, you can come to him and ask.
> I: So you're saying you're comfortable with Teacher #1-A?
> S: Yeah. (170611)

> I: Does Teacher #1-A going over and over the work make the class go too slowly?

S: Most of the time we appreciate it. Most of us don't get it the first time. He will explain how to do it 'til we understand. It don't seem like the class drag on; this teacher teach a good lesson.

I: How does the teacher handle mistakes?

S: We correct all our mistakes, even if it's a test, even if the grade is going in the book. Regardless, he say you can learn. You can make up any test you unsatisfied with.

I: What's a good grade for students?

S: It's like it's split. You got some who try they hardest and work up to Bs and Cs. Others say, "as long as I'm passing, it's okay." [My teacher] encourage you to reach the top.

I: You like that?

S: I do. (165611)

I: How do you get a good grade in this class?

S: Try your best, do your work.

I: Do you try?

S: If, basically, he see you need help and you don't say nothing, he say: "You not trying your best; you have to ask me." If you not doing nothing, he let you know he is doing this to benefit you in the future, and will give you a extension.

I: How well are you doing in here?

S: Right now, he say I am pulling all my Cs up to Bs. I been trying my best to do that. (157612)

Similarly, the replacement science teacher in School #4 was noted for her abilities to motivate students to do better, to encourage students to seek extra help, to help students when they did not understand a concept, to persuade students to work cooperatively to find solutions, to offer clear explanations for incorrect work, and to provide interesting activities in the classroom. Every student we talked to who had been in this class commented on the dramatic change in instruction and learning after the change in teachers occurred. Each was very clear about the benefits.

I: Are you ready for high school?

S: Yes, especially in science.

I: Why?

S: Teacher #4-A teaches us lots of different things and when teaching us, if we get a bad grade, she tells us to do better. She shows us what we did wrong. (421622)

S: We have fun. We are learning lots. (418622)

S: I'm learning all new stuff in science.
I: What makes you say that?
S: I've never done dissecting before. (414622)

Two of the students nominated this replacement teacher's efforts as their favorite class:

It's my favorite because the teacher does more things with us, like experiments. When the test come, you know what you're doing, and you get a good grade. (466621)

Now we got a new teacher. It's my favorite class. The teacher explains things to us. (461622)

Finally, a highly regarded math teacher in School #5, according to students, employed a set of signature actions that included: encouraging students to do more advanced work; offering after-school tutoring help (even before the school started its program); checking students' work and going over it until they got it right; showing students several different ways to solve a problem; and staying on students to complete their work. Below, students address each in turn:

I: Are you well prepared for high school.
S: Yes.
I: How do you know?
S: Teacher #5 talks about it. She says we're doing ninth-grade work.
I: How is that different?
S: We do more hard math, like geometry and equations. (529612)

I: What activities help you learn the most?
S: Math.
I: What is it about your math class?
S: It is the way she teaches us. It is real clear. And if we don't understand, we can come in after school. (501612)

The teacher shows us the work on the board and goes over it until people get it. (514611)

S: She show us tricks in there.
I: Tricks?
S: The teacher will give us like a hard problem and then will change it around, switch the numbers and make it a easier way—and a less faster way to do it.
I: What are you getting on your report card?
S: Last report period, I had a C or B. I brung it up from a D. (565611)

I think everyone should have a strict teacher like my teacher. We know there ain't no playing around. It's not a time to play. . . . You can finish high school if you have a strict teacher. (554611)

A final student was convinced that such actions were primarily responsible for her success in math.

I: Are you learning the same things you learned last year?
S: We're learning new math.
I: What do you mean?
S: We doing . . . what's that called? Doing integers, how to do common denominators.
I: You like that?
S: I like math; the teacher is teaching me more. So, if someone else needs help, I can teach them what I learned.
I: What grade are you getting in there?
S: B. (574612)

Although students highly valued the three teachers cited above, it was not difficult to find a set of similarly valued instructors in each building. In the next section we describe in more detail what made these teachers stand out in the minds of their students.

QUALITIES STUDENTS WANTED THEIR TEACHERS TO HAVE

There were at least six qualities, or strategies, or actions that students repeatedly discussed. They invoked these characteristics in response to a host of what we thought were distinct questions requiring somewhat different answers, such as what made a teacher a good one, what classroom activities helped them learn best, why they learned more and behaved better in some classrooms than others, what changes needed to be made in their schools, and why some students acted up in school? So prevalent and consistent were students' answers that we needed to do little analytical digging to ferret them out as major themes in the research. Each quality is worth investigating in more depth to convey an idea of what it looked and sounded like to the students.

Valued Teachers Pushed Students to Complete Their Assignments

> I prefer a teacher who makes sure I do it right. If they know I can do it better, I want someone who will push me. (327612)

This student's preference was typical of most of the students we interviewed. With rare exceptions, they wanted a teacher who nudged them along and made sure that they worked. Students felt that few of them had the confidence, drive, perseverance, or determination to do it on their own. They wanted and expected to be motivated to learn. And that unwavering push usually had to come from their teachers.

In the first year of the research, students continually used the word "strict" to describe teachers they thought were good ones. In subsequent interviews, we asked students to explain what they meant by this term and to give examples. Their elaborations indicated that they actually were talking about two phenomena. One had to do with academics and one with discipline. Students wanted teachers to make sure that they did their work **and** to make sure that other students did not disrupt the class. Exhibiting only one aspect of "strictness" rendered a teacher less effective than being able to marry the two. We separate our discussions of the two here only for clarity's sake.

For students, the desire to be prodded partially derived from a concern that they could easily slip into the habit of not doing work.

> It's not that I'm lazy, but I like a teacher that push me to learn. I might not be that confident at first, but then I'll get it. (270612)

> I like the ones that don't allow excuses. It's my turn to get an education. I need to have someone to tell me when I'm tired

and don't feel like doing the work that I should do it anyway. (332612)

If they don't keep after you, you'll slide and never do the work. You just won't learn nothing if they don't stay on you. (425621)

How teachers made sure that students remained on task varied. Sometimes the reminders took the forms of regularly checking their work and providing a visible and immediate accounting of which students were missing assignments.

S: She is always checking our books and our homework to make sure we're doing our work. (120611)

I: You said you prefer a teacher who makes sure you do your work? Why?
S: It shows that they are not there just for the money; they are there to help you learn.
I: Do you have teachers like that this year?
S: Yeah, I have one who keeps after me.
I: What does she do?
S: If I miss an assignment, she types up on a piece of paper what I am missing. (114611)

Not all reminders were formal or structured. Occasionally just re-iterating that students had ongoing assignments to do that night for homework was all it took:

I: How are your teachers this year about keeping after you to do your work?
S: They are good about staying after us. We are doing a career project now, and we have homework every day. Our teacher reminds us that we need to do it all the time.
I: Do you like that?
S: Yeah.
I: Is that being too strict?
S: No. (412621)

Students also praised teachers who would call their homes to make sure they were completing their work.

I: Why are you getting an A in reading when you did so
   poorly last year?
S: I work hard. She's hard on us. I like that. It's helping me.
I: What does she do?
S: She called my house and talked to my mom. (500611)

A teacher who stays on you is one who tell you to do your work,
call your house over and over and over, say "You're missing
this and that" and "You need to turn this in." (161611)

I: What do your best teachers do to help you the most?
S: [Teacher's name], she knows my mom real good. She stays
   on my back. She says she'll call my mom. (300611)

Such teacher actions, very close to nagging, seemed to nurture a
belief in students that they could be successful learners. This happened,
according to students, in a couple of ways. The first was by having
teachers act as cheerleaders and provide students with the general words
of encouragement that they could do the work.

I: Why do you say you prefer a teacher who makes sure you
   do your work?
S: They get you motivated to do your work.
I: What does your teacher say to you?
S: You can make it. You have to work hard. You need to do
   more than just have a C.
I: Why is that important?
S: I used to be lazy. I hated school. But I realized that if I want
   to apply for a job, I need my education. (414622)

I like the fact that she stays on students. Maybe they parents
are not on them. With the teacher encouraging me, it makes
me achieve more. (160612)

I: What do your best teachers do that help you learn?
S: She makes "bets" and "do's."
I: Can you give me an example?
S: She says: "I bet you can get an A. If you do this, I'll let you
   do that." You know, that kind of stuff. (326611)

Yet another way valued teachers instilled an attitude in students that they could succeed was by setting high expectations for the quality of the work and not letting students give up until they got it right.

    S: My English teacher, she makes you do better.
    I: What does she do?
    S: She gives you higher work. For example, our reading class level was low, but by giving us harder work, we are better. (104612)

    S: [My teacher] push me. I like that. He motivates me. He wants me to do good.
    I: How do you know that?
    S: He keeps pressing me until I get it right. (329612)

I like a teacher who stay on you until you get it done. (462621)

Regardless of how teachers specifically went about pushing students to do their work, the key for students was that there was someone who cared enough to make sure the work was being done and, through that caring, communicated to students that they were valued as learners.

    S: A good teacher is someone who stays on top of you and gives you homework. Someone who prepares you for the next grade. A good teacher cares about you.
    I: What do you mean by cares?
    S: If you don't do it, she doesn't just say it's on you to get the work in. (126611)

    I: What kind of teacher is most helpful to you?
    S: One who stays on your back.
    I: Why do you prefer that?
    S: 'Cause with that kind of teacher you know you're doing good, passing, learning, and doing more. (300611)

One of my teachers, she make you stay on your work; my other teacher, she don't care. She should be harder on the kids. The kids get on her nerves. (152612)

Valued Teachers Maintained Order in the Classroom

There was an "edge" to the atmosphere in all five schools. As students walked the halls and sat in classrooms, the potential for trouble bubbled just under the surface. As the old saying went, "The trouble with trouble is that it starts out like fun." Thus, a good-natured "bust" would morph into a challenging taunt, a playful put-down would turn painfully disrespectful, or a well-intentioned reprimand would evoke an agitated, aggressive response. The multitude of reasons students gave to explain why fights started implied that a youth would have had to be extremely vigilant to avoid triggering one. The list of fight-provoking reasons included: "he say, she say," "picking and someone gets tired of it," "showing off," "trying to rule," "bullying," "busting on someone," "talking about they moms," "looking at people hard," "being nosy," "calling someone names," "bumping into someone," "saying, 'excuse me'," "not saying, 'excuse me' (the tone made the difference), "getting revenge," "not being friends," "defending a friend," "not being from around my way," "feel they can get away with it," "cursing someone," "messing with someone," "not having no manners," "trying to prove something," "owing money," "think they big," and "stealing someone's girl (or boyfriend)." The hallways and classrooms teetered on the verge of emotional outbreaks and physical retaliation. This was the reality of education in the city.

According to students, teachers varied tremendously as to how well they were able to manage the ebb and flow of the tide of disruption. Some teachers seemed to spend all their time trying to "control" students. They yelled. They grew ominously quiet. They refused to continue lessons until the class settled down. They wrote numerous "pink slips," referring students to various administrators, counselors, and detention rooms. They sent misbehaving students out of the room. They concentrated only on the well-behaved students and left the others to their own designs in the corners of the classroom. They settled for an occasional and tentative order (i.e., quiet and still students) as the primary goal of the class.

Despite their apparent enthusiasm for disruption, an overwhelming majority of students greatly disliked being in such classrooms. A student on the honor roll at the school had this to say about the "bad" classes:

> It frustrates me to be in a bad class. The teachers need to punish the students better than they do. Like make a threat, but then they don't really go through with it. Sometimes they suspend students, but most of them like it 'cause then they don't have to come to school. (268611)

A student doing less well in school echoed the sentiment:

The kids don't do the work. The teacher is hollering and
screaming, "Do your work and sit down!" This makes the ones
that want to learn go slower. It makes your grade sink down. It
just messes it up for you. The teacher is trying to handle
everybody and can't. (263612)

In a logic peculiar to the young, they saw themselves as controllable
and willing to be controlled, if only the teacher knew how. Fortunately,
every single student had at least one such adept teacher and highly
valued the opportunity to be in those classrooms. They talked about a
variety of ways in which their teachers maintained order in the classroom.

> I: What should the teacher you described with no control do
> to change?
> S: Be like my other teacher.
> I: What is she like?
> S: She got that mean look.
> I: Tell me more.
> S: She have that attitude, like if you do something, you gonna
> pay for it.
> I: But the other teacher said that too. How is this teacher
> different?
> S: She don't forget nothing. She follow through on it.
> (451612)

> I: How can a teacher be strict?
> S: Like my math teacher.
> I: What does she do?
> S: She just know how to react to kids when they act up. Like
> say "be quiet" rather than "shut up." She call they parents
> too. (468621)

But students cautioned that teachers could slip over a vague and
undefined line that would result in a type of being strict that only exacer-
bated misbehavior.

> My teacher likes to do stuff her way. She like to get smart about
> it: "Y'all do it my way." She be telling us: "I pass [this] grade
> and I say do it my way or get a zero." But that makes students
> mad and they like to show her they're mad. (351612)

The comment seemed to suggest that teachers should be both strict and nice, something that thirty-nine students in the first year of the study said they preferred. However, some of those very same students pointed out that teachers could be too nice.

> It's hard for a teacher to be nice. Students figure if the teacher is nice, they can do anything. (373812)

This sometimes caused considerable problems. For example, the noise emanating from one particular class was distinctly audible before we rounded the corner to the corridor where it was located. As we approached, the din grew louder, unmarred by an adult voice straining to rise above it. Inside the class, the teacher sat at her desk, in huddled conversation with several students. She was unaware of our entrance until several other students shouted that she had a visitor. The sound level continued unabated as the teacher gave nodding permission for the study participant to leave the class. During the interview, the student described that brief episode as typical of most of the classes. The teacher would assign work, offer to assist any students with questions, and quietly wait for such requests. She would publicly praise each child who endeavored to work—never more than half—and would offer quiet suggestions to the others that they should do so as well. The student then summarized the situation and offered a solution:

> S: My teacher don't do nothing [to bad students] and she is too nice.
> I: What advice would you have?
> S: She should quit this job; it is too difficult for her. (380622)

Complicating the matter of being strict adroitly was students' insistence that discipline be fair. "Being fair" meant attending only to the students who deserved punishment.

> I am not treated fairly because the teacher blames me for stuff I don't do. (115611)

> Some kids get hollered at when they didn't do anything. The teacher punishes the whole class for a few. (228612)

> My teacher is strict. He always yelling at us and makes us do stuff we don't want to do. I prefer a teacher to be strict, but

not like that. He is always yelling at people when they not even saying something. (562612)

Students resented the "halo effect" as well, whereby the teacher would overlook the misbehavior of students who generally were good.

Teachers, thus, had to avoid being too mean, too nice, and unfair in dealing with students. They also, in some instances, had to not be too much fun.

> S: We act better in math and science 'cause the social studies teacher likes to have fun, to act like one of us. She'll joke around with us.
> I: What do you prefer?
> S: I would rather the teacher not joke around so much; kids take it to the point where they might not understand when to stop. (166611)

Thus, students, contrary to the worry that some of the teachers expressed at the outset of the study, separated a teacher's personal style, however engaging it might have been, from how well they taught the class. They tolerated skilled nagging and embraced adept discipline. The explanation for this, we think, lay in the students' using learning as the criterion for judging which actions they valued in teachers. Certainly that was the case with their preference for teachers' ensuring that they did their work. So too with discipline; students invoked academic reasons for why order was necessary.

> In a way, I do prefer strict. Teachers that just let you do what you want, they don't get a point across. Strict teachers gets the point across. (451612)

> I: Students are well-behaved in your math class?
> S: Yes.
> I: Why is that?
> S: We know, we realize we learned our math lessons. It's the class you just came in to get me out of. That's how we are in there. If we can't get it together, we can't graduate. (554611)

> I: What's your favorite class?
> S: Hers . . . cause I learn more things in there. (468621)

I want [a teacher] strict enough for me to learn. (270612)

The culpability of students in contributing to out-of-control class-rooms was undeniable. They were responsible. But they were not going to be the solution. They resolutely and irrevocably assigned that responsibility to the teacher. Thus, from the students' perspective, whether or not they learned remained a direct function of a teacher's ability to maintain order in the classroom. End of story.

Valued Teachers Were Willing to Help

While there was a swagger and exaggerated confidence in the students' social behavior and peer relationships at school, there was no such legerdemain when it came to students talking about their academic knowledge. They were quick to acknowledge that they did not know everything, even if they were hesitant to ask for help. Teachers who put forth extra effort and provided students with additional help received strong votes of appreciation from students. Nowhere was that captured better than in one student's account of a fellow classmate who had done nothing all year. According to the interviewee, the teacher's (Teacher #1-A talked about earlier in a couple of places) willingness to continually assist the recalcitrant student turned him around.

> S: One boy in the class, he do all his work now. If it wasn't for my teacher, he wouldn't do nothing. At the beginning of the year he don't do nothing; now he does. He wouldn't even take the SAT-9s; all he did was just bubbled in the answers.
> I: Why do you think that student is working now?
> S: Cause the teacher took time out to help him and talk to him. (106612)

The most meaningful way that teachers helped students was one-on-one, although this was difficult logistically for teachers. Most classes had more than thirty students. Even though we rarely saw more than twenty-five or so in class on any particular day, a fifty-minute class period left little time for an attendance check, a homework review, an assignment explanation, a bit of whole-class instruction, and then comprehensive one-on-one assistance.

Students, however, were understandably egocentric; the structural constraints of schooling mattered little to them. Despite the obstacles, students identified teachers who found a way to reach students individually.

    I: What activities help you the most?
    S: In math, it's showing us several different ways to do the problem. Also, tutoring one-on-one really helps. That way you get to spend more time with the teacher. (505611)

    I: What is a good teacher?
    S: It is someone who is always trying to help you out.
    I: What is the best way to help students?
    S: When they discuss a lesson with you one-on-one. (101631)

How, then, did some teachers manage to accomplish the seemingly impossible? One way that students mentioned was for the teacher to encourage students to seek before- or after-school help. In School #5, such help was systematically organized into the formal program described in chapter 2 in which many of the teachers participated, but there were teachers in all buildings who voluntarily extended their workday.

    S: I was getting Fs in September but I got my act together.
    I: What did your teacher do?
    S: She said she didn't want me to be left back.
    I: What did she do to help you?
    S: She suggested I get some tutoring and she did it. I come after school every Monday and Wednesday.
    I: How does that help?
    S: We get to do the work and learn how to study. (105612)

    I: What do teachers do if you don't understand something in class.
    S: If we don't understand, some will come over and say, "Here's my phone number; call if you don't understand." Others just say, "If you don't know it, it's on you."
    I: Which do you prefer?
    S: I like the ones that tell you, "I'm going to help you out."
    I: Why?
    S: Cause it make you feel someone care about you and that they not just working for the money.
    I: Don't you feel like they are nagging you?

S: No. You know what you gotta do; they just reminding you.
   (564612)

Help, to be valuable, did not have to be so structured as regular or even occasional visits to see the teacher before or after school. It was as simple as the teacher's finding a few brief moments during the regular lesson to stop by an individual's desk, or making the student comfortable with approaching the teacher during class breaks, or just stopping the whole class to see if they needed extra help.

S: I prefer the more involved teachers.
I: What do you mean by that?
S: You know, the ones that pull me aside, talk to me, are willing to help me out. (325611)

I: Are you having a good year?
S: Yes. I switched floors this year.
I: How did that make a difference?
S: The teachers are different.
I: How?
S: They be helping you more. If I ask a question, they show me how to do it. (332612)

A good teacher takes time out to see if all the kids have what they're talking about . . . and cares about how they're doing and will see if they need help. (369612)

Reaching out to students did not just mean spending time with them. Students also conceived of it as creating organizational arrangements that gave them second chances when they did not complete work on time.

I: What's a good teacher?
S: [Teacher's name], she's one who cares. She keeps you for detention.
I: What does she do?
S: She keep you after school and she calls your home.
I: Can you give me another example of how she helps you?
S: Yeah, over Christmas break she gave us all a piece of paper

with everything we did [all the assignments] from Sept-
ember through December. We got a chance to make up all
the work [we hadn't turned in]. Then she got tougher.
(111611)

Students recognized that offering extra help meant teachers
walked a fine line between a caring solicitousness and an overbearing
pushiness. But, on balance, they recognized that the extra help paid off
in the end.

I: What happens when you don't do your work?
S: My teacher try to help you understand it more. Most of the
time when they don't do it, it's cause they don't under-
stand it.
I: Is this how all teachers should act?
S: Yeah. They should do it for all people. Some kids can do it,
but don't want to. If the teacher pushes them, they can do
it.
I: Doesn't that sometimes make students mad?
S: Umhmm. They say, "Well, you ain't my mom." The teacher
say, "Then why do you come to school?"
I: Does that work for most of them in your class?
S: Yeah. (574612)

Another student pointed out the consequences of not receiving
timely help and, at the same time, highlighted the dilemma teachers
faced in having to accommodate student absences.

S: Say, for instance, I didn't come to school. The next day I
came in, they went over something new. There wouldn't be
like time to show me what they did. And the teacher
wouldn't make sure I understood. So, I start moving on
with them, but I be behind. They should have given extra
help.
I: When could they do that?
S: During lunch time. During class time they could let me
know the basic things. Then, when lunch time came, they
could pull me to the side and ask me if I want to do it. Then
it would be my choice. (385611)

Valued Teachers Went to Great Lengths to
Explain a Topic Until Everyone Understood It

A common student complaint was that teachers often moved through the material too fast, not taking the time to make sure that everyone understood it well enough to complete an assignment or take a test on it. Students therefore valued teachers who bucked that trend and would explain material thoroughly and repeatedly. Students talked about five ways in which good teachers did this.

The first was outlining, in clear terms, a set of steps for getting to an answer:

> I: What kinds of activities help you the most?
> S: When the teacher breaks it down, gives you every detail.
> (326611)

> I: What is your definition of a good teacher?
> S: Someone who knows how to break down explanations. Teachers who understand when kids have questions. (522611)

> I: Are you getting a good education this year?
> S: Yes.
> I: Why?
> S: I'm learning a lot.
> I: What are teachers doing?
> S: They feed it into our head real good. They do it step-by-step and they break it down. (526611)

The second way to explain things well was for the teacher to take as long as students needed to grasp the material, and not to rush to get to the end of the chapter by a certain time.

> I: Is school the same or different when compared to last year?
> S: Things are different.
> I: How have things changed?
> S: The teachers are real at ease. They take their time, you know, go step-by-step. We learn it more. It seems like they got the time to explain it all. We don't have to leave anyone behind. (533612)

I: Why did your math grade go from a D last year to an A this
year?
S: I didn't understand the teacher last year. [This year's
teacher] explains it much better.
I: What do you mean?
S: She stays on a subject for two days or until we know it for
the test. (102612)

I: What's a good teacher?
S: One who takes the time to explain things. [Teacher's
name] does a better job than the other teachers. She is
willing to take the whole class period to explain it, if we
need to. (120611)

Third, students bemoaned the fact that too often teachers' explanations simply mirrored the language of the textbook, which in many cases was quite foreign to them. What they found particularly helpful were teachers who taught a concept in alternative words to the textbook's explanation.

I: What activities help you learn the most?
S: I like to listen to the teacher.
I: Why is that so helpful?
S: Cause she puts it in her own words [rather than the textbook] so that I understand what it means. (401621)

I: Do some teachers explain things better?
S: Yes! [Teacher's name]. When we start a new chapter, he
always puts it in his own words. (411622)

Fourth, students lauded teachers who emphasized multiple ways of understanding a problem or completing an assignment. As we noted in the section on maintaining order, students were sometimes put off by a teacher's rigid insistence to do things solely "the teacher's way." Such behavior communicated insouciance on the teacher's part. So, in the eyes of these students, a teacher who explained well s also one who presented alternative explanations.

I: What activities help you learn the most?
S: Math class.
I: What is it about math class that is so helpful?

S: The teacher shows us several different ways to do the problems. (505611)

I: Is your teacher good at explaining things?
S: Yes. She talks about it both before and after we read a section from the book. (114611)

Finally, students acknowledged the value of providing a feedback loop to make sure students understood the material.

I: What kinds of activities help you the most?
S: When the teacher teaches you something and then asks questions [to make sure we understand]. (326611)

I: Why do you prefer a teacher who makes sure you do your work?
S: They take their time and they talk to you about it [the work]. They make sure you understand and know what you are doing.
I: How do they go about doing that?
S: They check everybody and explain it again if it is not right. They mark it and whatever is wrong they have us redo it for a higher grade.
I: Do you learn better by redoing your work?
S: Yes. You understand it better. (136612)

She tells us what we are missing [in our assignments]. She say she don't want a class of failures. She go over tests ahead of time and tells us what she expects of us. (121612)

Valued Teachers Varied Classroom Activities

As we discussed briefly in chapter 3, different activities appealed to different students. It was clear from our conversations with students that no one instructional strategy had uniform appeal. For example, some liked working in groups; others preferred working alone.

I prefer projects, doing group projects because they are more fun; and working in a group, you have more people to help you. (151612)

I prefer working in groups. You have more fun and you learn at the same time. You learn quickly. So, you have fun and you do work. But most of the time we be bored not in groups. (162612)

I prefer to work by myself cause most people don't read on the same level. I don't like to listen to others read. I might be ahead or behind where they are, whatever the case may be. (167612)

Some liked teachers to do most of the talking while others wanted to play a larger role in the activity.

I prefer the teacher to talk to us and then explain it. (261611)

I: What kinds of activities help you learn best.
S: When we listened to Shakespeare on tape, then we created a talk show program where we talked about it and took up sides like the Jerry Springer show. We even had a brawl! Also, our teacher dresses up as "granny grammar" and takes on a different personality. She talks about different grammar rules, like compound sentences. She makes it funny and we remember it better. (123612)

My favorite teacher is one who makes her lessons relate to people my age. Like we might do plays where we acted out a story. When kids do stuff together, they learn that way. (377612)

And, some liked highly structured lessons and others preferred discussions.

S: My favorite subject is math 'cause she made our work into games and I caught on real fast doing it that way.
I: Can you give an example?
S: Okay, with graphing. She made all these games out of graphs. She had worksheets for it. Had all the directions for it on the paper. But I don't like doing it in groups.
I: Why?
S: Cause I get irritable and you sit there and argue for half an hour when you could just go to the teacher and get help. (264612)

I prefer discussions mostly. You get more out of it. The more
talk we have together, the more we go over things, the more
we learn. If you have an experiment and don't have a discussion about it, you wouldn't know what you're doing. (263612)

Projects, lectures, real-world connections, groups, creative acting,
individual work, games, and discussions were all preferred ways of learning. No one strategy was likely to be a surefire success in a class with all
students. Thus, varying activities appealed to more students and, therefore, kept more students interested.

S: I don't have no favorite class. I don't like none of them.
I: Why?
S: They boring.
I: What makes them boring?
S: 'Cause we don't do something that's fun.
I: What makes something fun?
S: When you do different activities. (150612)

Valued Teachers Respected Students, Related to Them,
and Tried to Understand Their Worlds

I heard teachers talking about people, saying "Those kids
can't do nothing." Kids want teachers who believe in them.
(264612)

Students applauded teachers who did more than just pass along
content to them. They especially appreciated teachers who made the
effort to understand and believe in them. That was commonly accomplished in one of two ways. The first was for teachers to take the content
students were learning and make it relevant to students' lives.

S: I like it in reading when we talk about real-life stuff.
I: Why is that helpful?
S: 'Cause it makes me more aware of stuff going on. (325611)

S: Instead of just writing lots of stuff [notes off the board], we
   have conversations and discussions.
I: What kinds of things do you talk about?
S: He talks about government—how it is around the neighborhoods. (329612)

I: What are you studying in social studies?
S: We are learning about Mesopotamia.
I: Is that interesting?
S: Yes.
I: Why?
S: Cause the teacher makes it interesting.
I: How does she make it interesting?
S: She tells us stories about her life there. That makes me
   want to learn about the past. (500611)

Establishing a connection with students' lives went beyond using
relevant content. It also meant taking an interest in students' daily lives. A
couple of students expressed this well: "I like someone who puts themselves into our shoes" (129612), and "I guess a teacher don't got to be
nice, but they got to be respectful." (161611) Even if adopting this attitude was difficult for teachers in the context of how students treated
them day in and day out, students claimed that a teacher's respect ultimately made them want to learn.

S: [The teacher] gets us prepared for the future and tells us
   not to go down the wrong road.
I: What does he do?
S: He relates to us. Instead of talking proper English, he talks
   about why people be busting on each other. He says it is a
   way to say I love you. (315612)

Sometimes a teacher don't understand what people go
through. They need to have compassion. A teacher who can
relate to students will know when something's going on with
them. If like the student don't do work or don't understand,
the teacher will spend a lot of time with them. Some teachers
do the lesson one time and expect you to catch on. (165611)

A good teacher to me is a teacher who is patient, willing to
accept the fact that she might be dealing with students who
have problems. (160612)

S: My math teacher is a pretty good teacher.
I: Why?

S: Since this is one of his first year's teaching, I give him credit. He relates, but he also teaches. With some students, he tries to get them to work and he tries to communicate with them.

I: What do you mean by communicate?

S: He jokes around and he laughs and he'll get in our conversations. It's sort of rude but it is good in a way too. He advises us. He not only tries to teach but gets involved with us. (453622)

BEHIND THE ACTIONS: THE STUDENT–TEACHER RELATIONSHIP

Students seemed to equate the above teacher actions with "caring." That is, their quotes indicated to us that students were continually making inferences about where they stood with their teachers and whether teachers had students' best interests in mind, to use Noddings' (1992) definition of caring. Were they important enough to be pushed, disciplined, helped, taught, and respected? If so, then teachers valued them; if not, then teachers had given up on them.

The six qualities of teachers students wanted to have, therefore, took on an importance far beyond the specific instances in which they occurred. Their cumulative presence apparently led students to construct an image of certain teachers as truly interested and invested in enabling students to succeed. Students perceived that such teachers accepted no excuses for failure, that the teachers would go to any lengths to make success possible. Essentially the students naturally zeroed in on a phenomenon central to effective urban education that researchers have labored to depict for years—the quality of the relationship between inner-city students and their teachers (see Delpit, 1988; and Ladson-Billings, 1994).

Examples in which students paired teachers' actions with more global attributions of teachers' concern for them and their learning can be found in many earlier sections. In this section, we want to call attention to student–teacher relationships formally as a means of underscoring the significance the students attached to teachers' preventing them from shrugging off work and, thereby, learning.

We illustrate the point with a diverse group of students from a single school to convey the extent to which students at all performance levels valued teachers who took the time to prevent failure. Remember that our sample within each school cut across academic and behavioral performance. Thus, being able to draw on a wide range of the students from a school increased the likelihood that the students shared the expressed attitudes regardless of their standing in the school.

Three students from School #3 illustrated the manner in which they invoked "caring" as the primary motivation behind a teacher's actions.

I: Are you getting a good education?

S: Yes, because my teachers this year say, "Pay attention; next year is going to be harder." They be like, "Come on, you can do good."

I: Do you like for teachers to be like this?

S: Yes, it tells me they care.

I: What do you mean by "care"?

S: Say if a teacher just sits down and says, "I don't gotta teach you." They just trying to get money. If they pat you on the back, that's a good teacher. It shows they want you to do good. (358612)

I: Do you like for a teacher to push you to do your work?

S: If you don't do your work, you ain't gonna get nowhere.

I: So you like for them to nag you?

S: Uh-huh.

I: How does that make you feel?

S: Better.

I: Explain.

S: I know [he or she] cares about me getting a good education.

I: Do they all care?

S: Some do. (361611)

One of my teachers really push kids to do work. She is the most caring teacher. She really want you to do work. Sometimes that make me mad but I still try to do the work. It nice to know you got a teacher who cares.
(353612)

It appeared that believing a teacher cared about them did more than just make students feel good. Students in the school transformed teachers' caring enough to "teach" them into academic self-confidence. Five more of the students in the building offered comments on this development.

One male explained: "[When they push me] it makes me think I can do the work; I'm glad they're trying to teach me instead of ignoring me, thinking I can't do it." (368611) Another agreed that such actions, "gives me confidence to do my work." (355611)

In response to our query about what it took to be a successful student, a third one stressed that "all students need people who are there for them." (363611)

A female looked at this topic from the other side of the coin. She argued that with the students in her school, "The teachers have to push them or they will give up." (369612)

A fifth student in the school went to some length to describe the effect that a particular "pushy" teacher had on him:

> It made me feel more comfortable, knowing that I'd be able to know the work. See, at first, I didn't like her subject. At first, I didn't do no work. I thought it like any other class where the teacher would not make sure you know what you're doing. But my teacher was like "you want a F, you want a F?" She kept getting on me. I like that. (385611)

As the above student claimed, a teacher who accepted no excuses often meant the difference between success and failure. When left to their own devices, some students worked hard to **not** do their work. They knew when they could cut class and still blend in with hall traffic to escape notice; and they would strategically calibrate their classroom effort to navigate the boundary between an F and a D. These actions were possible as long as there were cracks in the system through which students could slip.

The "no excuses" teachers closed the cracks. For example, one student discovered this late in his eighth-grade year when a teacher to whom the student had not been assigned asked to have the young man moved to his class for all of the major subjects. The teacher had had the student two years earlier and was disturbed by the student's obvious efforts to avoid going to classes in eighth grade. The teacher explained to us that the student could do the work but was successfully managing to avoid doing so. Rather than complain about the teacher's close supervision, the student praised him.

I: What is the best thing about this school?
S: My teacher.
I: Why?

S: He teach and he don't play. Other teachers they play and
let you play. My teacher tell you what you got to do. That is
why I come to school now—to learn.

I: So, you're saying the teacher stays on students?

S: Yes. He stay on your back.

I: Do you prefer that?

S: Mmhmm.

I: Do you feel ready now for high school?

S: Mmhmm.

I: How do you know?

S: 'Cause I know how to do stuff now. (365611)

Students in each of the other schools expressed this same line of
reasoning—that "no excuses" equaled caring which led to increased self-
confidence in doing schoolwork—equally adamantly and in similar
proportions.

It is important to point out, again, that students were able to separate qualities in a teacher that they just liked from those that helped them
learn better. In other words, students, like the following three females
from School #5, could distinguish between a teacher's individual style or
demeanor and a teacher's instructional style.

S: My teacher is serious.

I: What does that mean?

S: It mean like he don't play around; he always have a straight
face.

I: Do you like that?

S: I don't like it, but it is good that he that way. He teaches us
about life that way. (582612)

In that classroom—we all say she was the meanest teacher;
but I bet you, you will learn something in there. She will force
you to learn. Even if I say to her "Stop bothering me," I like it. I
still want them to be nagging me. (578612)

She's mean out of the kindness of her heart. It's for a reason:
So we can learn. (556612)

To us, examples such as the above ones clearly exemplified the
depth of students' appreciation of the value of their relationships with
their teachers. They were not so superficial as to only praise the "cool"

teachers and roundly ridicule the more stern members of a faculty. Instead, their reference point for judgments about teacher quality was whether they learned and whether the teacher ensured that they did. Good teachers would not give up on them for any reason. They felt that teachers who pushed them to work also believed they could complete the work.

The above quotes suggested that students began to believe in themselves, as well. It was more than coincidental that students so often associated this approach with "caring" or, more tellingly, with simply "teaching." Teachers who continually pushed students to do their work became known as those who "cared," or who "actually taught," or "did their job."

It is not enough, however, in the context of reform to highlight the qualities of a few exemplars working against great odds in difficult situations. Indeed, too many stories of success in American urban education are descriptions of "pockets" in which a teacher or a team of teachers succeeded in Don Quixotic fashion. For the Philadelphia School District's reform efforts to truly have had an impact, such pockets would have had to be extended to encompass an entire school. Otherwise, the quality of a student's education would be left to the luck of classroom assignments and not educators' systemic efforts to improve schooling. As long as what was truly noticeable to students about their classes was their uneven instructional effectiveness, then Children Achieving's supposed early success would ring hollow.

FIVE

SPREADING THE POCKETS OF SUCCESS

The overall reform goal in Philadelphia was to ensure that all students learned challenging content in a timely manner. To do that, students had to be in classrooms in which learning was possible on more than a hit-or-miss basis. Thus, whatever else the reform accomplished, it would have to at least "scale up" the pockets of success our students described to encompass a whole school.

Another way to phrase what we mean by "scaling up within a school" is to think of it as reducing the significant variations in instructional quality that existed across the classrooms in the five Philadelphia middle schools. The chapter 3 classrooms in which students experienced little pedagogical accommodation to learning styles and discipline-defined best practice, encountered a watered-down and below grade-level curriculum, and claimed the atmosphere was not amenable to learning needed to move in the direction of the types of exemplars described in chapter 4. Moreover, classroom interactions and activities would have to become infused with the "no excuses" belief, so that this improved instructional setting could actually benefit all classroom residents, not just those students who already motivated themselves or had adequate support outside school. Indeed, as the students argued, if a student's success on a task depended on resources, support, and assistance that were not provided within the school's walls, then the task was sure to result in failure for some. Success for all students, then, would require school-wide attention to the quality of their instructional experiences, including students' relationships with their teachers.

Such a development was not noticeable to students in the five schools. We feel that the presence of occasional pockets of effective middle school teaching reflected the routine comings and goings of teachers in Philadelphia more than the intentional effects of Children Achieving. However, it was possible, though not probable, that a natural variance in students' educational preferences would have caused them to make comments similar to those in chapters 2–4 no matter what had happened under Children Achieving. Students, in other words, had always disapproved of what some teachers did and simply continued to do so in the interviews. Their personal biases therefore blinded them to aspects of schooling that reform had touched, rendering students as inappropriate data sources on improvement progress.

It was not completely clear to us what teachers in the five buildings had done in response to Children Achieving and so we were not in a position to say whether they had implemented changes that should have shown up in student talk. It made sense then to locate a middle school serving a similar population of students in which it was known that substantial instructional changes had been made and to interview those students about their classroom experiences. If their descriptions of uneven instruction and wasted learning time resembled the other students' in both type and frequency, then we would have to conclude that students were suspect informants on whether reform had actually touched classrooms. On the other hand, if students' answers differed significantly from the comments in the previous chapters, then we would be on firmer footing in asserting that the prior students' accounts accurately reflected little change and that talking with students was a productive means of assessing the depth of Children Achieving's reach.

Addressing this issue was important to us. Even though we felt that what students had to say about teaching was worthwhile information for educators to consider, this benefit alone fell short of the presumption that the ways in which students talked about classrooms could validly serve as indicators of a reform's effects. Thus, PEF made it possible for the research to include a sixth school, one that had been working with a major R&D center for several years on goals entirely compatible with those of Children Achieving.

It was rewarding to find that students in this school, in fact, did describe teaching and learning differently from the students in the other five schools. The students noted increased instances of teaching that enabled them to learn, and they experienced more consistency in the instruction and content they encountered. Their comments validated students as potentially valuable sources of evidence about reform progress—and at the same time hinted at the abundance of resources that the other schools would need to engender similar responses in their students.

A major portion of this chapter provides student-based evidence that the long-term partnership between the R&D center and the school improved both the consistency and quality of students' pedagogical, content, and classroom environment experiences. The remainder of the chapter uses the District's and the R&D center's quantitative data and anecdotes from students we interviewed—who serendipitously had attended both School #6 and one of the other five schools—to examine the value of the changes the school had made.

A BRIEF DESCRIPTION OF SCHOOL #6

The students at School #6 were economically similar but ethnically more diverse than those at the other five schools. Forty-six percent of the students were Latino, 26 percent African American, 15 percent Asian (primarily from Southeast Asian countries), and 14 percent Caucasian—with a significant number of the latter being Arab Americans. The school's attendance boundary touched on the edges of the catchment areas for two of the other five schools, so differences in neighborhood housing and economics were modest. In fact, the percentage of students from low-income families was in between the low 80 percent figure for School #1 and the low 90 percent for the other schools.

School #6 was organized similarly to the other five. It had SLCs, within which students were assigned to two- or three-teacher teams for the major subjects. However, there were a couple of important differences. First, the school spilled over to an annex building where one-third of the students remained for the entire day, creating a "school within a school feeling" for those students. Second, nearly half of the teaching teams used a looping approach wherein the students and teachers were able to spend at least two years together. Separate research in the school on this practice pointed to benefits: more caring on the part of teachers, higher use of research-based instructional practices, and increased student effort (MacIver et. al., 1999).

Most notable was the school's partnership with an educational research and development center housed in a major university. Through this federally funded program, in its third year at the time of the study, teachers became involved with long-range instructional planning, extensive professional development, and standards-based curricula in all four of the major subject areas. The program also included a once-a-week career exploration program to expose students to future career options and examine career attitudes and interests.

STUDENTS' ASPIRATIONS AND TEACHERS' PREFERENCES

Although the students were more diverse ethnically that those in the other five schools, there was little to distinguish them from their counterparts in terms of their future plans and their preferences for classrooms that supported learning. Like their peers, School #6's students planned to finish high school, attend college, and find work in their preferred occupations in numbers that far exceeded what the hard statistics about urban youth would predict.

The students were certainly no less optimistic about their educational futures. All but two of these eighth graders (96 percent—fifty-five of fifty-seven who were asked) had plans for post-secondary education. The students were equally confident that they eventually would be able to obtain satisfying, high-status occupations. Their selections of professional (doctors, lawyers, and sports) and trade-related work (hairdressing, owning a local business) mirrored those of their peers in the other schools, with the exception of a somewhat greater interest in computer-related careers.

Also, like the students in the other five schools, those in School #6 mentioned the same teacher qualities detailed in chapter 4 as being central to a teacher's effectiveness: (1) "staying on students" to complete assignments; (2) controlling student behavior; (3) providing extra help; (4) explaining material and assignments clearly; (5) varying activities; and (6) respecting students. There was not much of a difference in terms of the frequency with which they talked about the characteristics either.

What was different, however, was the degree to which they described these characteristics as being regularly present in their classrooms. Instead of wistfully naming these qualities as ones they would like to see their teachers develop or highlighting them as welcomed exceptions, the students tended to ground their descriptions almost exclusively in their current situations. Thus, in describing the routines of their classroom, the students portrayed much greater consistency in pedagogy, content, and classroom environment than was the case in the other schools, as the following discussion illustrates.

Pedagogical Differences—The Case of Science

The approach to science at School #6 began with a set of broad questions. What is science? What do scientists do? How do scientists go about answering their questions? The instructional program focused on these guiding issues as a way to combat students' ideas that science was not a subject in which they could do well. In the words of the school's science coordinator, "science is a hands-on, minds-on affair." Students had weekly lab activities chosen to illustrate the role of science in students' everyday lives and the world beyond. To ensure ample time to explore important scientific principles, the schedule permitted students one double period of laboratory science a week. In addition, all students participated in the District's annual science fair exhibition.

The curriculum included a series of science kits. Each kit addressed a specific theme related to earth, life, or physical science and promoted inquiry-based learning and contained all the necessary materials for students to work with to conduct their investigations. The topics and tasks were aligned with both the national science standards and the new Philadelphia standards. Technology was integrated with the science program through research assignments, word processing, graphing, and special Internet projects.

The difference between students' pedagogical experiences in science at School #6 and the other five schools was the hands-on nature of what they did, both in terms of frequency and type. Indeed, experiments (or, in one case, what students described as "projects") were a regular part of the science regimen as students uniformly participated in a double period of science once a week. Students, therefore, referred to labs as routine, which was a marked contrast from students in the other five buildings who almost without exception viewed experiments as occasional, sporadic, or even nonexistent activities.

We do lots of labs and projects. (603612)

Instead of staying in books, we get to do hands-on things, like experiments. That's more interesting. The book is boring. (618641)

We do labs every Thursday. The teacher makes us show step-by-step how we did it. We have to write up our labs and she hands them back on Monday. (604611)

As did students in the other buildings, School 6's students regarded hands-on work as a valuable way to learn.

I: Do you do much lab work?
S: Yeah, we work on them two or three times a week.
I: Does that help you learn better or not?

S: Yeah.

I: Why?

S: It's better than just writing stuff down. You get to learn by doing.

I: Can you give me an example?

S: Yeah. We were learning about contaminated water and we had to test thirty-six different water samples. (605611)

I: What do you do in science?

S: Every Thursday we do a double period lab.

I: Is that helpful?

S: Yeah, it helps me see what the book is talking about. It is better than reading about it. When you do it, you understand. (616612)

They commented that they were learning both science and how to be a scientist.

S: We just finished a "how to do" project.

I: What did you do?

S: I explained how to do hair rollers.

I: How did that help you understand science?

S: A part of science is being very clear about all the steps you follow in your experiments. We practice that by clearly going through the steps of a regular activity. (625612)

While students described experiments as fun, we did not hear more than one or two talk about them as activity for activity's sake. This partly may have been because teachers used regular science class time to prepare for and then follow up on the labs. As the following student noted, the lab did not end when the materials were put away:

S: We have a double period every Tuesday where we do a lab. We also have homework with the lab.

I: What do you do for homework?

S: We usually have to write a one-page summary where we answer four questions: What did we do in the lab? What did we like about it? What do we need to do to improve? Would we do it again? (611651)

The students generally portrayed textbook use as being subordinate to hands-on activities. They still read the books and took notes on what they read, but texts appeared to serve mostly as reference books from which to gather background information about lab topics.

> We keep a notebook where we keep our notes from the textbook and our worksheets. But most of that is work related to our labs. Almost all our work is related to the lab. (620612)

> We only use the textbook for research. (610652)

> We are always doing research. Every week we have a project where we go to the computer to find information. (612622)

Putting textbooks into their proper place in the modern science classroom, a final student concluded:

> I: Do you use the textbook much?
> S: No. We are way past that. (627621)

It was not surprising, therefore, that we found a high degree of enthusiasm for science throughout the school, and not just from students who had a particular teacher.

> S: It's exciting and fun.
> I: Why is it fun?
> S: Every day is a new thing! (606621)

> We have lots of fun. All we do is projects where we try and understand how variables affect each other. Everyone understands what we are doing cause we do lots of hands-on stuff. We also sing and dance in there. The teacher comes up with songs for things that helps everyone remember stuff. (610652)

Compared to students in the other five schools, then, nearly all of the students in School #6 talked about doing hands-on—often investigative—science. They also placed greater emphasis on the role of the scientist, an aspect of the subject that hardly any of the other students raised.

Content Differences—The Case of Writing and English

In the reading/language arts program, students received two periods of reading/language arts instruction (100 minutes) every day. The R&D center's staff trained teachers in a whole language approach that was literature-based rather than basal-oriented. Teachers integrated reading and writing, relying on a regular set of prescribed activities to do so. These activities included:

- **Partner reading:** students read a section of the book first silently, then orally with a partner.
- **Treasure hunts:** students searched for and wrote answers to questions about a book's plot, literary devices, and the writer's style and technique.
- **Word mastery:** students practiced saying the new vocabulary words aloud with their partners until they could say them accurately and smoothly. They also wrote "meaningful" sentences for each new vocabulary word—that is, elaborated sentences that provided context clues to the new word's meaning.
- **Story retelling:** after reading a passage and discussing it with their partners and with the class, students were expected to summarize the main points to their partners.
- **Story-related writing:** after reading a section of a book students were given special prompts that required them to write a brief composition about what they had just read.
- **Extension activities:** variety of cross-curriculum assignments used writing, research, fine arts skills, and interdisciplinary projects to explore themes and ideas from a story.
- **Tests:** students were expected to respond to a mixture of analytical and detail-oriented questions about the story's main issues, write meaningful sentences for selected vocabulary words, and read aloud passages to the teacher or another adult.
- **Explicit instruction in comprehension strategies:** students received instruction in identifying main ideas and themes, drawing conclusions, making predictions, understanding figurative language, and so on.

The consequence of the school's having an established, focused curriculum in language arts was a remarkable unanimity among the students about definitions of what it meant to "do writing". Almost all the students described writing as a frequent, creative, and constructive act. The students, thus, shared a common understanding and acceptance of writing as a process, one that entailed planning, execution, revision, and critique.

I: What activities help you learn the best?
S: When we do pre-writing.
I: What is that?
S: Its when you organize what you want to say. (605611)

I: What do you do in RELA (reading, English, and language arts)?
S: We are writing about four days a week. We usually write to some writing prompt. The teacher give us some examples with a Venn diagram. We follow the five steps of the writing procedure. And most every day we are working with other students on writing. (626612)

I: What do you do when you write?
S: We begin by constructing a web—only for major projects.
I: What happens next?
S: Then we go through several drafts.
I: How many drafts?
S: We usually do a first draft, a second draft, and then a final copy. (603612)

S: Every time we read something we write about it.
I: What do you write?
S: We retell the story. Usually we write a summary of two or three paragraphs. We also have to answer "treasure hunt" questions. And when we write something we correct it, revise it, and change with a friend to correct it again.
I: How many times do you rewrite most things?
S: Mostly about three times. (624631)

I: Are you getting better at writing?
S: Yes.

I: How do you know?

S: We have to keep rewriting things and if we get it wrong he makes us do it again. (607612)

We always write and then we go over each other's work. (610652)

Adhering to the process seemed to have had the teachers' desired effect. Students described writing as communication and assessed it as an invaluable skill to develop.

I: What do you have to do to get an A on a writing assignment?

S: You have to do lots of rewriting, like changing words and sentences around. It is important to be clear. If you write too much, you might not make sense. (612622)

S: I learn more in RELA.

I: Why?

S: I like writing.

I: What makes writing so interesting?

S: When we write we are learning to make it sound better each time we rewrite it. (623642)

The emphasis on communicating was mostly missing in the other schools. Students in those buildings viewed writing more mechanically, as a rule-bound endeavor. Communication loomed large in School #6. For example, the students explained that including details was important because they "let a person get the point" (652612) and would "make a person understand what something looks like" (656621).

Certainly writing constituted a significant portion of the school day at School #6. Students said that they were expected to write daily and that writing was integrated with their other language arts experiences. But even more important, writing was also stressed in the other subjects, particularly math and science.

We write every day, usually to some set of prompts. We just finished some historical stories. Yesterday we did a retelling of *Norma* [an opera they had seen downtown]. (602612)

S: For science homework we usually have to write a couple of paragraphs about our experiment.

I: What do you write about?
S: Did we enjoy the experiment? What did we do? What did we find? (613651)

In math class our teacher grades our journals and he makes us write reports. That is the first year that math has not been all numbers. (611511)

The students in School #6 shared a more singular definition of what it took to write well. Their remarks emphasized writing's purpose as communication, with the role of correct grammar, sentence structure, and organization being the means to accomplish this rather than the end themselves, as was the case elsewhere.

A Note on Mathematics

Although math instruction was not a part of the data presentation on the five schools, it is worth noting that the program in School #6 emphasized algebra for all rather than just for the top students. This math program was an effort to respond to the national reform movement in mathematics, emphasizing problem-solving and authentic tasks. Every eighth-grade student had algebra. In preparation, the fifth and sixth graders used *Everyday Mathematics* and the seventh graders had *Transition Math*. As with the other content areas, the program's onset included intensive staff development and follow-up support for teachers. It also featured a "double dose" extra-help component for students who were in danger of not being able to keep up with the daily instructional pace. These students received a combination of computer-assisted instruction and structured cooperative learning to reinforce their regular math content (MacIver, Balfanz, & Plank, 1998).

Classroom Environment Differences

Few students in School #6 described being in classrooms where little if any learning took place. To the extent that they noticed classroom-to-classroom contrasts in student learning and behavior, the comparisons tended to be between major subjects and particular exploratory classes that had a tradition in the school as the place where students regularly misbehaved.

We asked a subsample of the students to talk about classroom situations in which students behaved better or worse and how these differences affected their learning. Two-thirds of the students with whom we explored this issue said that they were better behaved in some classes than others, about the same frequency as in the other five schools. However, School #6's students maintained that the disruptive classes were in the exploratory subjects. Exploratory subjects—art, family life, music, and so on—tended to be troublesome in all of the schools. As one student explained, "Students will act up if they think it is not an important class" (652612). The problem at School #6, according to the students, was that the teacher of one of the subjects was "too nice" and, as a result, the teacher "can't control 'em" (663611). In contrast, the teachers in the major subjects, according to one student, "usually don't allow distractions; they tell us to 'settle down' and if they see something, they speak up and jump on it right away." (654621)

There was disagreement, however, among several students about the classroom environment in one major subject. A student we talked to claimed that peers in the class rarely behaved and that little was accomplished. The very next student we interviewed identified the class as his favorite, but hinted that perhaps all was not going well:

> My teacher's class is different. That's why I like it. He help us a lot—how to sit, how to talk, stop using slang. We free in the classroom to do what we want. He teach us how to be on our own when we get older. But he not talking to us anymore. The class was talking too much. He gave us enough work to do, he hasn't given up. He just want to show us "if you want to talk, I'm not going to teach." (666611)

A third student in the class attributed the problems to the teacher's technique, comparing it to the perceived more thorough preparation of the other teacher on the team, but concluded that it was still possible to learn in the class:

> The teacher, he don't have things planned out. He'll give out the work and forget it. He will tell us our research is due and then won't remind us. My other teacher, they all scared of him. They will talk real loud in his class but he can get us quiet; it takes awhile. But if we don't get quiet, we get the consequences. But I can learn in the other class too; it is just kind of loud. (667612)

Thus, students described the teacher as not strict enough in the control sense. However, they all indicated that he still pushed them on academic matters, especially with writing. With that, the students reported they understood that successful writing required multiple drafts and that the teacher consistently expected this to happen.

Importantly, students in the school expressed varying degrees of satisfaction with their major subject teachers, yet almost every student indicated that class time was productive. This represented a dramatic departure from what we found in the other five schools, where nearly every child could identify an entire major subject or a significant portion of the school year in which little of substance occurred.

EVIDENCE OF SCHOOL EFFECTS

School #6's students characterized their school as having much less instructional unevenness than did their counterparts in the other five schools. However, not only was there greater consistency in pedagogy, content, and environment, but there also seemed to be a greater emphasis on mastering challenging content, at least to the extent that the curriculum offerings were developed from the current national standards of what students should know and be able to do. School #6 had educators throughout the school, therefore, that closely approximated the teachers that students had established as exemplars in the interviews.

Were School #6's students any educationally better off than their counterparts in the other five schools for having had more teachers like this? We ask this question not to validate the R&D center's intervention in School #6 so much as to validate students' collective wisdom about the kind of teaching that enabled them to learn best. If the answer to the question was in the affirmative, then students' opinions about good teaching had considerable merit.

We had three different forms of evidence that were relevant to the question. The first was students' reactions to their schools as a whole; the second was standardized test data collected by the School District and School #6's R&D partner; and the third came from several students who had actually attended two of the other five schools in the study prior to coming to School #6. The comments from these latter students, although the most anecdotal, were perhaps the most telling because they were able to provide a comparative look deep inside the schools.

We must point out that, in a sense, students in the five schools contradicted themselves. On the one hand, they felt their middle school had prepared them well for the future while, on the other hand, they readily identified major subject classes in which little, if any, learning occurred. The former opinion did not seem to be compatible with the latter; and the latter should have tempered the former. Our only explanation was that the students had little to compare at the school level but had experienced numerous contrasts at the classroom level. In the absence of information to the contrary, they were unwilling to be generally negative about the school as a whole. Their limited prior knowledge, coupled perhaps with a natural egocentrism, could have constrained their ability to think critically and holistically about education. They had a rich storehouse of classroom experiences, however. Thus, it was concerning teachers that students were the most expert observers.

Students' Perspectives on School #6

It would be difficult to argue that students in School #6 were any more or less satisfied with their school than the students in the other five were with theirs. All the students tended to be extremely positive about the quality of the education they were getting and how prepared they were for high school. With little basis for comparison, and despite complaints about certain classes, the students in all the schools were satisfied customers.

The students in School #6, however, were able to provide numerous examples of classrooms in which they learned. Their descriptions were similar to ones the other students provided, but they differed in their ubiquity. So, the valued teachers in School #6 pushed, helped, explained, and so on, just as they did elsewhere. There simply was more of them.

> My teachers, they pursue you. If you do something wrong, they on your back. They tell you they gonna help you, they tell you they want you to do good. (673612)

> My teacher make you do work. She will help you if you don't understand. Then she will check it, see how you doing it, and see that you doing it right. (655632)

> Most of the teachers teach. They don't try to put you down. They want you to learn. If we need help, they can give it until we understand it. (656621)

> The teachers really care for you. They make sure you get a full understanding. They keep asking, "Do you get it? Do you want me to do it again?" (659621)

Students also described a school where life seemed more orderly. Classroom disruptions were limited to the exploratory classes for the most part, and the overall tone of the hallways seemed less contentious—at least to us as we wandered the halls. Thus, it was possible, as students had occasionally hinted in the interviews, that misbehavior was sometimes the product of frustration in class and that good teachers taught in a way that encouraged students to pay attention.

As we mentioned, School #6 had a more diverse student body. Perhaps for this reason, the issue of ethnic tolerance arose in the interviews here. There was evidence that the greater diversity in the student body had become the basis for the students' learning tolerance rather than inciting conflict. For example, an African-American male volunteered that he "hangs with the Arabic kids." When asked why, he said: "They're funny; they crack jokes; they take me places." (604611) An Arabic female commented: "The students are all like best friends here; we all get along." Her explanation was that, "We just like each other; we hang out during lunch and gym, even though none of them live near me." (608642) A Caucasian female suggested that, "There is a good mix by race here; we are a really tight clique." (610652) A Latina female offered: "I hang with the black kids [because] I like anyone who gets along with me and they do." (612622) And, finally, an African American female maintained that she liked school because "There are lots of different races and they teach me different things; they are very friendly." (616612)

Tolerance seemed to carry over to settings where, in the other schools, control was fragile. In an assembly, one of the SLCs produced and performed the "Harlem Renaissance," a topic the students were studying in the social studies and RELA classes. The students introduced this historical movement as having three components: literature, art (visual and performing), and dance. They then demonstrated these over a one-hour period by reading key passages of literature, singing, dancing, and acting. Even a teacher got into the act by playing a rousing piano rendition of "Let My People Go" that drew loud applause from the audience.

To us, the young audience appeared captivated. Although teachers were scattered throughout the room, there was little need for them to intervene to correct the students' behavior. Perhaps the most telling incident was when one of the performers froze and completely forgot his lines. Rather than laughing, one student member of the audience called out: "That's OK." Those words of encouragement gave the young man confidence to start again. With his eyes now clenched in concentration, he got halfway through, only to freeze again. No one laughed or shouted a catcall. Instead, a rising crescendo of spontaneous applause arose from the audience, diffusing what could have been a debilitatingly awkward moment. The performer walked off the stage, slightly embarrassed, but not the least distraught.

Student Performance Data

The majority of the students said that they learned and behaved well in School #6. We thought it would be interesting to see if quantitative data about the school reinforced this portrait. Information was available from both the School District and the R&D center.

The School District's Children Achieving initiative included a new accountability system that systematically tracked student achievement across three benchmark grades (grades four, eight, and eleven) for three major subject areas (reading, mathematics, and science). The District chose the Stanford Achievement Test, Ninth Edition (SAT-9), as the primary assessment tool. It assessed literacy, problem-solving, and critical thinking. Students at the three benchmark grades had been tested annually since the 1995–1996 school year. The results of these tests were reported as a percentage of students who scored in the advanced, proficient, basic, and below basic categories. The long-term goal of the District, by the year 2008, was to have 95 percent of the students achieving at least at the proficient level.

An analysis of the most commonly reported numbers, the percent of students performing at or above the basic level, indicated that five of the six schools showed growth from 1995/96 to 1997/98 in reading; four of the six produced improved mathematics performance; and all of them reported gains in science. School #6 did not show gains significantly greater than the other schools. On the other hand, using as the metric for analysis the percent of students reaching proficient status or above (the primary target of the District), students in School #6 outperformed students in the other five schools in reading and science, but not mathematics.

The R&D center staff also conducted test result analyses with the mathematics items most closely aligned with the program being implemented at the school. They found that relative to a matched sample of students in other schools, the students at School #6 who received extra help produced significant gains in mathematics performance (MacIver, Balfanz, & Plank, 1998). Positive classroom-level findings were also found for reading comprehension (MacIver, Plank, & Balfanz, 1997).

However, these quantitive findings must be interpreted with great caution. The testing program was still relatively new, and the District's desire to test all students and its inclusion of the percentage of students taking the test as a factor in a school's overall assessment confounded the scoring early on. For example, some schools had fewer than half their students taking the test during the baseline year and almost all the growth those schools reported over a two-year period could be accounted for simply by increasing the number of test-takers, without ever improving the quality of instruction.

Another reason to sprinkle a few grains of salt on the test data was the simple fact that the overall proportion of students achieving any degree of success on the tests was low for all of the six schools relative to the entire District. Moreover, in reading, rarely did half of the students perform at the basic level in any of the three test years; and in the other two subjects, rarely did a quarter do so. Pogrow (1998;1999) has argued, therefore, that teasing out program effects in such a situation has little merit because absolute high scores and large, rather than modest, gains should be the hallmarks of effective programs.

Finally, although achievement test scores were firmly entrenched as indicators of the quality of instruction in the Philadelphia School District, this status was as much a political consequence as an educational one. Indeed, numerous missiles have been launched to attack the logical flaws in using tests such as the SAT-9 as proxies for quality (Koretz, 1992; Popham, 1999). These arguments are persuasive to us and call into question whether much can be said at all about the relative merits of the schools' instructional programs based on students' test scores.

We delved into this topic briefly merely to say that School #6's students were decidedly more affirming of the school's efforts than were the more "objective" measures. The reader is left to determine which indicators had greater weight. What was heartening to us actually was that the subjective and objective estimates differed. This suggested that students were in a position to provide nonredundant information. In the case of School #6, students portended greater achievement down the road; in the cases of the other schools, they cautioned that any substantial, **instruction-caused** test score improvement was unlikely, in the absence of other changes being made.

Student Comparisons of School #6 with the Other Study Schools

Serendipity allowed us to interview five females and one male at School #6 who had previously attended two of the five original schools in the sample. Therefore, we were able to solicit, firsthand, the differences they had encountered between the two schools. Their observations reinforced signs of a different instructional tone to the school that were alluded to earlier.

Two of the females we interviewed spent time at School #3. When making comparisons between the two schools, their comments revolved around the nature of the work, the standards set for the work, teachers, and their peers. With respect to work, both commented that it was more difficult at School #6 than at School #3.

> S: The work is challenging.
> I: Do you like doing hard work?
> S: I like doing work that is on my level. The work here is much harder than at School #3.
> I: Was School #3 too easy for you?
> S: I was beyond the work at School #3. Here the work is much harder and more like what I can do. (603612)

> School #6 teachers start you at your level and then move you up. School #3 teachers start you too low. (615612)

In answering a follow-up question about the difficulty of the work, both students made a point of talking about how strongly they felt that their work was tailored to a grade level above them:

> In algebra they give us ninth-grade work. Science is also ninth-grade work. In reading, we are reading at a ninth-grade level. (615612)

> I: Are you doing lots of review work, or are you learning new stuff?
> S: We did some review early in the year but now we are doing mostly ninth-grade stuff. Our teachers consider us ninth graders. That's what they tell us.
> I: How is that different?
> S: We are doing more work. In fact, we are doing work that even ninth graders wouldn't know.
> I: Can you give me an example?
> S: Yeah, like in RELA, we are learning about speeches of language.
> I: What kinds of speeches?

S: We know about things like personification. (603612)

A comparison of experiences in science classes illustrated well the difference in instruction:

I: What do you do in science class?
S: We got to pick a project and we wrote a book on that topic that could be used to teach a six to eight year old about it.
I: What did you pick?
S: The solar system. We also have science labs during our double period.
I: Do you do more in science than at School #3?
S: There all we did was read the book! At School #6 we do experiments and have science contests.
I: Do you use the textbook much at this school?
S: No. (615612)

In addition to differences in the work students had to do, comparisons inevitably came around to teachers. With respect to the latter, both students claimed that the teachers at School #6 were much closer to the "no excuses" mode that was described in such detail in the previous chapter. Teachers at School #6 reportedly showed more caring or empathy for their students:

S: The teachers pay attention to you more. They want to know your problems. They talk to you more. I used to be bad. But now I have someone who cares.
I: Who is that?
S: The teachers.
I: What do they do?
S: If I have a D on a test, they want to know why. They talk to us about our work. Also, the teacher here tell you you can do it. At School #3, I had to do it on my own. At School #6, they are here to help me more.
I: When do you get help?
S: Before school. I come every other day at 7:15. (615612)

I: What is a good teacher?
S: A good teacher is someone who listens to your ways and lets you make your own mistakes.
I: Do teachers do that here at School #6?

S: Yes, teachers are good about that here. They are better than the ones at School #3.

I: Why is that?

S: At School #3, the teachers can't contain the students.

I: Who is responsible for that difference—the students, the teachers, or the school?

S: It's mostly the students. They are just better educated here. (603612)

This same student went on to talk about how the teachers at School #3 always seemed to be preoccupied with disciplinary matters, and therefore were unable to use much of the class period for teaching.

S: At School #3, they spend so much time with the bad kids, writing pink slips and giving detentions, so there is less time to teach. Here the teachers don't make you work. It's more on the student. They don't stop for those who don't want to learn. At School #3, I was always getting suspended.

I: How do you behave here?

S: I stay out of trouble. I got all "1s" on my report cards [for behavior]. I am much better than at School #3.

I: Why?

S: The teachers talk to us here and tell us about the importance of graduating and being ready for high school. They say we are no longer kids, but instead are adults; and in high school [teachers] won't give us second chances. (603612)

Both female students also referred to important differences in the standards at the two schools. This seemed to be a result of both individual teacher behavior and a more general school philosophy. One student commented about the standards in the classroom not being clear at School #3 while being crystal clear at School #6. The other student referred to standards in terms of the recognition the school gave to students.

In order to get an A in RELA [at School #6], you need to read three books, do your logs, write in your journals, and have some graded prompts. It was not real clear what you have to do at School #3. (615612)

They just pile on the homework and projects at School #6. At School #3 they used to give us lots of awards, but most of the kids didn't deserve them. Here, they have higher standards and they don't give out as many awards. (603612)

Finally, the conversation also naturally fell to making comparisons about the students in the two buildings. The differences were striking.

S: At School #3 they [students] are rambunctious. They also like to stop others from doing their work. Here they are more sophisticated. They do their work. They are also more willing to help others.

I: Why is that?

S: I guess it's because they know it and they are just nicer. Here they are more sensitive about other cultures. Kids would really tease a Vietnamese or Cambodian student [at School #3], but they don't here.

I: Why not?

S: I don't know. Maybe because they teach us to be nice and the kids are not violent. (603612)

S: At School #3 the kids don't care.

I: Why?

S: It's a neighborhood school, and you just follow your friends. If the teacher don't tell you, you don't learn.

I: What would happen if students went from School #3 to School #6?

S: They would change [that is, treat one another better].

I: What would happen if students went from School #6 to School #3?

S: They would not change [that is, adopt bad habits of students at School #3], but they wouldn't be able to change [that is, make better] the other students. (615612)

In this final comparison, one of the girls talked about how students reacted to hard work at both schools, and how the attitude of their teachers influenced that reaction.

I: What happened at School #3 when kids encountered hard work?

S: They give up.

> I: What about at School #6?
>
> S: We try.
>
> I: Why?
>
> S: They teach you so you think you can do it. At School #3 they just give it to you. (615612)

Three females who had previously attended School #4 had similar reactions to their experiences in the two buildings. Most notable to them was the difference in student behavior. With respect to School #4, they said:

> There were more fights there. It was in a bad neighborhood. (651622)

> The students were more wild. (658622)

> At School #4, the people were so bad. People were always talking. The surrounding neighborhood was bad. (664642)

Such was not the case at School #6.

> The students here are more calm; but the neighborhood is becoming bad. (651622)

> It is more quiet here. (658622)

> The school is graffiti-free; it is a clean environment. The students have manners; they cooperate. This school is much better. (664642)

Apparently there was a connection between the overall atmosphere and what went on in the classrooms, as two of the students mentioned.

> The teachers here give a break to you. They explain it to you if you don't understand. (651622)

> The teachers here care if you learn. Like if you don't do your homework, they make sure you stay after and get it done. I'm like learning in all my classes. (664642)

For this last student, her lack of learning was the reason she left the previous school. Both she and her parents "thought I didn't learn anything; this school [#6] is much better."

One of the Latina students felt the comparison between the two schools was a little more complicated with respect to learning. She could not speak English when she entered School #4 and was able to be in a Spanish-only class in that building. For that reason, she was able to get "straight As" on her report card. In School #6 she was thrust into English-only classes, with an occasional visit to an ESL resource room. For her, then, "everything went down; they were teaching at a higher level and everything was English; and I was, like, 'Oh, my God!'" Fortunately for her, a support net was in place. When asked how she managed to pass, the student explained:

> My teachers said if you don't know how to do something, ask. They said, "We want you to pass." They said, "We're gonna help you do your work." They was interested in me learning. (658622)

The student proudly finished her story:

> Now I know more. I'm not falling asleep in class. I did that because I had no idea what was going on. So that's why now when you come into my class, you'll see me awake. (658622)

A fourth student we talked to, a male, did not attend School #4 but had visited it and School #6 when his family had moved to the city and was trying to determine which school he should attend. His brief assessment pointed to the fairly obvious differences.

> School #4 was not like so [made a smooth motion with his hand]. It looked like people were not learning; they were all out of their seats. This school [#6] is much better. (669641)

STUDENT TALK AND SCHOOL DIFFERENCES

The teachers in School #6 had taken part in considerable staff development. Students in the school recounted experiences that suggested that, in comparison to the other schools, there was much greater consistency in pedagogy, content, and classroom environment and that the teaching and content, in science and English at least, were in line with current national thinking. Students, therefore, triangulated the school's and the R&D center's impressions that important changes were underway. The students, however, were decidedly more positive about the school's effects on them than were objective measures. They were greatly comforted by having strict, caring, and helpful teachers in the classroom and felt that this translated directly into increased learning.

Whether or not being in a school with more "pockets of success" would show up more dramatically in the future on the District's standardized measures of achievement remained to be seen. However, it was safe to say that the students tested at School #6 had had access to similar educational experiences within their building whereas their counterparts in the other schools had encountered much more varied instruction. The educational differences certainly seemed significant, even if the statistical ones did not.

At an educational level, School #6's students mirrored the others in desiring teachers who stringently refused to allow them to fail. Rather than being left to their own motivation and ingenuity to navigate eighth grade, they were surrounded with skilled and concerned adults who wove themselves into a safety net. In this regard, the program the teachers had implemented seemed to have had important benefits. Our purpose in studying it, however, was not to evaluate the program ourselves but to see if students could tell the difference between it and the instructional circumstances in the other schools. Collectively they did.

We think the case of School #6 made an analogous case for supporting teachers in their improvement quests just as students were supported in the classroom. To simply say to teachers "Do more" would be similar to demanding that students try harder as the sole means of increasing their chances to succeed. Moreover, leaving teachers largely on their own to raise student achievement would demean the extraordinary level of effort each workday required of every teacher, regardless of their adherence to a "no excuses" philosophy. School #6, with its professional development opportunities, its curriculum development work, and its cultivated climate of doing quality work served as a safety net for teachers. Fortunately, a plentiful storehouse of ideas, assistance, and materials greeted them at their wit's end, which were resources teachers in the other schools desperately lacked.

Six

STUDENTS AND REFORM

The students in our study expected to succeed in life. They planned to graduate from high school, go to college, and have satisfying careers. Moreover, they were entirely trusting that their schools had prepared them to accomplish these goals. Statistics said they were wrong; and the students themselves were able to describe gaps in their education that were setting the stage for failure. However, students were also able to identify teachers' actions that promised to counter the many daunting obstacles they would encounter: an academic push, stern discipline, extra help, clear explanations, varied activities, and thoughtful relevance. These actions were the concrete manifestations of a "no excuses" philosophy that made student success the schools' responsibility, especially in those circumstances in which children and/or their parents were not in a position to handle the responsibility themselves. As mentioned earlier, the "whole point of it," one of the students explained, was "to keep you from failing."

We cannot emphasize the astuteness of this comment enough. It was not the individual practices but the overall purpose that was critical. Laundry lists of "effective practices" have been around for a while yet we still continue to see stark, frightening, and stubborn disparities between the achievement of poor children and their wealthier peers (Hedges & Nowell, 1999). We contend that something else is missing in recipes for urban reform: an underlying belief that all children can succeed and that it is the schools' responsibility to ensure that this happens.

"All children can succeed" has become the rhetorical banner of current reform efforts. In other research we have conducted that included students, teachers, and parents, we have found that nearly everyone espouses this belief but that they often attach qualifiers to it (Corbett, Wilson, & Williams, 1999). Some educators say "all children can succeed . . . if they make an effort;" others say "all children can succeed . . . if only the parents would help;" and still others, fewer in number, assert "all children can succeed . . . and it's my job to make sure they do."

It is this latter interpretation that students in this study found to be so valuable to their learning. Teachers who adhered to it tried everything they could to teach students; and when those efforts failed, they tried something else instead of shrugging their shoulders and saying, "You can only do so much."

We think that this philosophy must infuse all efforts to improve urban education. We hesitate to assert this position so strongly because it places the burden for student success so squarely, and unfairly, on teachers' and administrators' shoulders. After all, they are not the only residents in the urban village; and they all already work very hard, enduring minimal instructional resources (Kozol, 1992), large classes (Tomlinson, 1990), and absent colleagues (Pitkiff, 1993). But life is unfair, especially in big cities, and students identified a host of teachers who managed to act as if they were the last resort of hope for students. These were the same teachers who the students claimed enabled them to do their best work in school. It was not a coincidence. Good teachers mattered; and the students spoke nearly in one voice about what a good teacher looked like in their urban middle schools.

We are making a rather global claim based on the remarks of less than a couple hundred kids. However, the unanimity with which the students spoke about what they valued in the classroom was convincing to us—and probably not unique to just these urban middle school students. For example, the Philadelphia Education Fund, in its effort to disseminate results from the study within the District, created a poster for classroom display with illustrative quotes concerning the qualities of the "no excuses" teachers they wanted. The posters found their way onto our refrigerators. One of us asked his thirteen year old about the accuracy of the set of qualities. With a disdainful, matter-of-fact retort of which only adolescents are masters, she said, "So what's the big deal about that; that's what we all think."

Our bent for qualitative research makes us prone to accepting systematically gathered anecdotes as evidence of widespread events. However, there were notable similarities between our students' thoughts about their educational experiences and those of the students in Wasley, Hampel, and Clark's book (1997), *Kids and School Reform*, which is the most contemporary work that closely sought the same purposes as ours. Specifically, in the latter, the authors emphasized the importance of classroom routines and a teacher's repertoire, of a teacher's caring and expectations, of rigor paired with innovation, and of scale and discourse. Those phrases sounded like labels for phenomena much like having order in the class, introducing a variety of activities, connecting classwork to students' lives, and demanding that they complete school tasks. The match was not perfect, but definitely in the same ballpark, especially given that Wasley et al.'s group of students was much older than ours.

Still, Wasley, Hampel, and Clark talked to no more students than we did and chose to highlight only a handful in their book. Our recommendation, therefore, is for the reader to **not** take our word for it. We think the better idea would be to ask students directly. Whether one is a teacher, administrator, parent, interested citizen, reformer, or educational researcher, just ask the kids what they think. They have plenty of thoughts to share. *Look Who's Talking Now* (Kushman, 1997) contains concrete descriptions of ways that schools have obtained information from and about students to guide and assess reform efforts.

This chapter amplifies our advice that students are worth listening to. We first draw several implications for enabling district-wide reform to have a noticeable presence in the classroom, based on the students' comments. After all, the only path to greater academic achievement that is open to all students is the one they and teachers travel daily together. Second, we argue that there has to be a place in the process of reform for students as participants, not just as beneficiaries. They may not understand the political ins and outs of reform, but they can at least partially help to clarify what reform should accomplish and how well it is accomplishing those goals. Moreover, they will need opportunities to adjust and accept new roles akin to what teachers and administrators must have as they undergo reform.

Making Reform Noticeable

We do not want to stray too far from "the wisdom of youth" in this book. We think their simple and succinct messages can stand on their own merit and that what students had to say has direct implications not only for Children Achieving but also urban school reform generally, especially in those settings in which the educational community regards students' motivation as one of the primary obstacles to improvement. Students, however, only see a small piece of the reform picture. It is an adult task to take the lead in translating their ideas effectively into reality. In that vein, we have several thoughts, expressed in the form of recommendations, about how reform efforts such as Children Achieving can best take advantage of students' experiences.

The intention behind all the recommendations is to engender changes that are "noticeable" in the classroom. We have chosen that word deliberately to add texture to the idea that meaningful reform must alter the teaching and learning process. Children Achieving, like many change initiatives, aspired to this goal and yet assiduously eschewed putting in place anything more than indirect mechanisms to affect and detect what went on in classrooms. For example, teachers received training but little, if any, in-the-school assistance in implementing that training. The School District established school performance measures that could be construed to be artifacts of instruction such as attendance and test scores but none that depicted actual classroom activities. Thus, the District could only infer that reform had penetrated to this level from the inputs it provided and the outputs it saw. The classroom itself remained opaque.

Reform's being noticeable is doubly important with high-stakes accountability because research has demonstrated, and common sense suggests, that it is possible to raise test scores without improving the educational process (Koretz, 1995; Popham, 1999). Teaching to tests that are poorly matched to the curriculum, narrowing instruction to focus almost exclusively on test content, and manipulating the population of students who actually take the test are all time-honored means of influencing test results that have dubious merit and that occasionally emerge in stressful testing situations (Heubert & Hauser, 1999; Popham, 1998; Wiggins, 1999).

The only people who are in the most advantageous position to determine whether anything at all of worth has occurred in the classroom are its residents; and of teachers and students, only students have the additional advantage of being able to compare one classroom to the other regularly. They need not know anything about what is going on school- or district-wide, but what they notice about their experiences can speak volumes about the effects of those larger activities. To us, **"noticeable reform" denotes alterations in the daily classroom routine that are apparent to students and/or apparent from the way students talk about school.** Therefore, the following recommendations are based on what students had to say about school and are intended to enable reform to have the greatest potential for actually being noticeable to them.

Focus Professional Development on Adults' Underlying Beliefs about a School's Role in Supporting Student Learning Rather Than Discrete "Best Practices"

In our opinion, teachers' refusal to accept any excuses for failure separated the classrooms in which students succeeded from those in which they did not. It was not so much that a teacher adhered to a couple of the qualities that students wanted present in their classrooms but that the teacher, according to students, acted out of a sheer determination to promote success.

We have no doubt that most of their teachers knew that they should encourage students to finish their assignments, that they should give clear explanations of tasks and concepts, that they should give assistance whenever they could, that they should vary classroom activities, that they should maintain an orderly class, and that they should relate what students were learning in school to the outside world. All those actions can be found in numerous places in the literature on urban education (see, for example, Williams, 1996). However, even if a teacher tried to adhere to current thinking about best instructional practices, students in these schools would still fall through the cracks unless the teacher also believed that it was his or her responsibility to construct a supportive net to catch them.

Good instructional practice would increase the likelihood that more students would understand their work and be willing to do it; but, more important, the "no excuses" philosophy ensured that a teacher would not accept helping **more** students as a proxy for helping **all** students. In the schools we visited especially, if students were free to fail, many would. In other words, limiting the schools' responsibility to a "we do the best we can, but it's really up to the students and their parents" approach was simply another way of dooming large numbers of students to failure.

"No excuses" has become an increasingly popular phrase to refer to the overall approach of schools and/or teachers who have succeeded in enabling low-income students to perform well in school. For example, Carter (1999) conducted case studies of "no excuses" principals who led "high-performing, high-poverty schools" and found that they had seven common qualities. These principals were free to make financial, organizational, and educational decisions; established measurable challenging goals; relied on a cadre of "master teachers" to stimulate faculty improvement; emphasized test-taking skills and test results; connected student achievement and discipline as mutually reinforcing characteristics; worked closely with parents to help them help their children with schoolwork; and challenged teachers, students, and parents to continually work hard. Regardless of the specific elements of a "no excuses" strategy, wherever the term is used, it conveys the integral role that educators who do not give up on any students can play in the educational lives of children and youth who have traditionally not performed well.

Improving pedagogy and the quality and consistency of subject content would indeed be progress in the five schools, as it was in School #6. The schools would become better in a professional technical sense. However, shaping adults' beliefs about the need for additional support would represent true reform. It would alter the assumptions behind teachers' actions and spur the creation of classroom environments in which every child enrolled in the regular instructional program could find the encouragement, discipline, help, explanations, variety of activities, and connections to their lives necessary to achieve.

Emphasize the Quality of the Relationships between Teachers and Students

Caring, defined as acting in the best interests of others (Noddings, 1992), was intuitively recognized by the students as teachers refusing to allow them to fail. They interpreted how a teacher taught as an indication of how the teacher felt about them as students. Teachers who taught, cared; teachers who did not teach did not care. There was nothing technical about instruction. For students, every action the teacher took was relational. It was all about relationships, as Wasley, Hampel, and Clark (1997) convincingly convey.

The Philadelphia reforms were not much different from those proposed elsewhere for urban students in terms of reducing the sheer numbers of students that adults would encounter daily. Certainly we would not argue that reduced class size, small learning communities within buildings, and looping were ill advised. These may even have been necessary companions to creating productive relationships, but they were not sufficient. Lower numbers meant fewer relationships to build, but the relationships still had to be built (Ross, 1999). Students' descriptions of the teachers they wanted to have collectively painted a portrait of teachers who become deeply involved with student learning. Small classrooms were not necessarily better if the teachers in them still accepted failure. It was the quality of the relationships in the classrooms that determined the educational value of the setting.

Changes in Student Performance Standards Must be Accompanied by the Creation of Standards for Pedagogy, Content, and Classroom Environment—and the Professional Development Necessary to Implement Them

The Philadelphia School District instituted standardized measures of student achievement to assess an obviously "unstandardized" education for students. This seems unfair. Students in some classes had better chances to be instructed in ways that accommodated their learning styles than did students in other classes. Students in some classes encountered entirely different content than did students in other classes in the same subject in the same grade in the same school. Students in some classes had more opportunities to learn than did their peers in other classes in which discipline was absent. We doubt that Philadelphia was much different from any other school system in this regard. Indeed, widespread inconsistencies in educational quality stimulated the national discussion about scaling up reform (Elmore, 1996).

The lesson from School #6 was that establishing expectations about and providing training for how a subject should be taught, what should be taught, and the kind of classroom conducive to learning could create much greater consistency and closer adherence to discipline-based definitions of good practice in the instructional program. While these changes may not have shown up immediately in the District's standardized test scores, School #6's students' high degree of involvement in investigative science and their sophisticated understanding of the complexities of writing clearly underscored that desirable educational benefits were present to a greater degree than in the other study schools. Of course, School #6 received an incredible amount of outside support. Just as teachers, according to students, should not fail students who had no chance of succeeding unless they had extra help so too low-performing schools should not be punished by an accountability system unless they have had access to substantial support.

Connect Changes in Standards to Grades, Not Just to Performance on Large-scale Assessments

Standards were for the adults in Philadelphia; grades were for the kids. One would have wished for some degree of congruence between the two, but it was grades, not district-devised performance indices, that students relied on to gauge their progress. In the previous pages, grades popped up as a central ingredient to students' notions about how to get to college and secure a satisfying career. In our previous reports to the Philadelphia Education Fund (Corbett & Wilson, 1997a; 1997b), grades were a major reference point for how students defined the extent of their success in school. Put simply, grades were endemic to students' notions about how they were doing in school.

What this means, we think, is that standards would have to be thoughtfully and uniformly connected to report card grades if they were to have meaning for students. For example, being able to be an A or B student and performing below the "basic" level on a standardized test would seem to be an irreconcilable contradiction in measuring academic performance, assuming the test was worthwhile in the first place. Careful and thorough attention would have to be given to what each individual teacher expected of his or her students and how consistently these expectations were communicated and reinforced from classroom to classroom. Within, and across, school conversations about expectations and grades, therefore, would have to find a prominent place in professional development activities.

An overall discussion of the connection between course grades and performance standards would also serve another important purpose. While we continually have praised students for their insights—perhaps to the point of annoying hyperbole—noticeably absent in their statements was much attention to the quality of their work. They incessantly talked about "doing work" as a key to success; the thought that merely doing the work could not be enough was rarely mentioned, except in conjunction with a couple of demanding teachers. Students would have benefited greatly from clearer ideas about what quality meant. Well-defined standards that were clearly reflected in grading practices would have enhanced the District's attempts to emphasize excellence.

Create "Extra Help" Situations That Encompass All Students Who Need It, Not Just Those Students Who Avail Themselves of It

As more students had access to caring relationships with adults, then—and only then—should the District redefine the level of acceptable work. Students would not automatically meet redefined expectations without increased opportunities for extra help. The Philadelphia School District acknowledged as much several years into Children Achieving. The superintendent argued in a public plea for increased state funding that to make it tougher for students to pass from one grade to the next without providing adequate instructional support for doing so would do no one any good.

In all the schools, students could identify a teacher who would provide additional tutoring or a couple of afternoons where after-school help was available. This, of course, was entirely discretionary; it had to be voluntary when such help fell outside the regular school day. However, School #5 had managed to establish a discretionary *and* formal after-school program that was involving an apparently large number of students. Certainly it was more systematic and thorough than an individual tutoring program. School #6 altered its schedule to give students extra time in science and English and created an in-school "extra-help" program in math. According to the students, these efforts were extremely effective.

One of the ironies of schooling has always been that while educators acknowledge that humans learn at different paces, schools have been organized as if the opposite were true. Short class periods, a "paced" curriculum, grade levels, and standardized testing schedules all ensured that these students, many of whom required more time to learn, would perform poorly. For a variety of reasons—the stigma of being "held back," an inconveniences for families, and a lack of resources to name a few—this contradiction between understandings about learning and the practical exigencies of running a universal system of education would not be resolved soon, if ever. The only alternative was for the District to have increased the amount of extra help available within the school day to students who desperately needed it to compete with students who had more resources at their disposal. Thus, efforts such as those at Schools #5 and #6 should become a part of the "no excuse" support net in all schools.

Extend Extra Help Beyond School Work to How to Succeed in the Future

We were convinced that students were able to be so specific about what they valued in teachers because they had had such extended experience with them. Their simplistic, almost platitudinous, plans for securing a desirable future was the result of the opposite—little familiarity with the paths to high school graduation, college, and jobs. The students claimed that success in high school and college was the ticket to adult happiness. They had either internalized the message well, or at least knew that others expected them to do so. Unfortunately, they knew little about what they should do to act on it.

Students reported that few in their families had attended college, but that going there was a prominent wish of family members. Unfortunately, the schools did little to compensate for this lack of firsthand information. The consequences could eventually prove to be dire, as illustrated by George Weiss's Say Yes program in Philadelphia. This philanthropist promised 112 students from a feeder elementary to one of our study schools full financial support for college. Periodic newspaper accounts documented the difficulty of students' taking advantage of that offer, mostly because of their lack of understanding and preparation for the challenging demands of college (see, for example, Mezzacappa, 1996).

As evidenced by Furstenberg, Nield, and Weiss's (1999) study of ninth graders in Philadelphia, falling by the wayside occured early. Thus, there was a pressing need for the middle schools to broaden and deepen students' experiences with, and understandings of, the worlds of higher education and work.

REFORMING WITH, NOT FOR, STUDENTS

Nearly everyone in the reform arena claims to be in it "for the kids"— from entrants in local elections for school boards to national politicians crafting new legislation. Their good intentions, however, often ignore the fact that the ensuing changes will require students to change as well. Just because the above implications are based on students' stated preferences does not mean that students will willingly and easily add new expectations to their existing definitions of what school is supposed to be like. Discrepancies between how youth currently act as students and how they will be expected to act as the consequence of reform will affect their acceptance of change, as it does with adults.

Unfortunately, students are not often considered to be important actors in the change process. As Fullan (1991:170) observes:

> When adults do think of students, they think of them as the potential beneficiaries of change. They think of achievement results, skills, attitudes, and jobs. They rarely think of students as participants in a process of change and organizational life.

The distinction between students as "beneficiaries" and "participants" is significant. Using the image of a beneficiary obligates adults to improve the educational system with the best interests of students in mind. Using the image of participant demands that young people become directly and formally involved in reform activities before and during the implementation phase. The former is better than not using any image of the student role in reform at all, but the latter represents a more potentially meaningful and powerful impact on students' classroom lives.

Our research shows that students had significant, nonredundant information to contribute to the Philadelphia School District's assessment system. The quantitative data contained evidence of modest test score improvement in all six schools. This finding could have been interpreted in any number of ways: that extra resources had not done School

#6 much good; that Children Achieving was having a positive effect in five poor schools; that Children Achieving was a weak reform at best. The students said that the quality of instruction in School #6 was evenly distributed throughout the building and congruent with current thinking about the major subject areas. They said that instructional quality was tremendously uneven in the other five buildings as was the curriculum. These insights would argue against racing too quickly to judge School #6 negatively and would argue for pouring greatly needed additional professional development resources into the others. To dismiss the R&D center's and School #6's efforts and to "stay the course" in the others would be wrong, according to students. Direct evidence to support such conclusions was available nowhere else in the District.

If one accepts the proposition that students have a claim on being participants in the process of reform—by virtue of their unique perspectives on schooling and the necessity of their changing just as the adults must, then one also has to acknowledge that to date every reform effort has violated what the literature on change recommends as elements of an effective improvement process. That is, students do not have formal opportunities to work out the meaning of change for themselves, to receive technical assistance in trying out their new roles, or to obtain formative feedback on how they are doing. Change takes years for adults to comprehend and digest; it "counts" for students immediately, in terms of new promotion rules, graduation requirements, and performance standards. Instituting accountability systems early in the reform cycle has perhaps given adults a taste of what the fruits of the change process look like to students all of the time—foreign and bittersweet. Fullan (1991:170) reminds us:

> Educational change, above all, is a people-related phenomenon for each and every individual. Students, even little ones, are people too. Unless they have some meaningful (to them) role in the enterprise, most educational change, indeed most education, will fail. I ask the reader not to think of students as running the school, but to entertain the following question: What would happen if we treated the student as someone whose opinion mattered in the introduction and implementation of reform in schools?

We know what would happen. The adults would see what their actions look like through the eyes of the people who matter most. They would obtain thoughtful insights about effective instruction and its distribution within schools. They would understand that students desire to be educated as much as, if not more than, the adults want them to be. They would find out that they have invaluable partners in the educational enterprise—if only students had the chance.

REFERENCES

Ainsworth-Darnell, J., & Downey, D. (1998). Assessing the oppositional culture explanation for racial/ethnic differences in school performance. *American Sociological Review, 63*(4), 536–53.

Allen, E., & Lederman, L. (1998). Lessons learned: The teachers academy for mathematics and science. *Phi Delta Kappan, 80*(2), 158–64.

Bodilly, S. (1998). *Lessons from New American Schools' scale-up phase: Prospects from bringing designs to multiple schools.* Washington, DC: RAND Corporation.

Carter, C. (1999). *No excuses: Seven principals of low-income schools who set the standard for high achievement.* Washington, DC: Heritage Foundation.

Cervone, B. (1998). *Walter H. Annenberg's challenge to the nation: A progress report.* Providence, R.I.: Annenberg Institute for School Reform, Brown University.

Christman, J., Foley, E., Passantino, C., & Mordecai-Phillips, R. (1998). *Guidance for school improvement in a decentralizing system: How much, what kind, and from where?* Philadelphia: Research for Action.

Corbett, D., & Wilson, B. (1995). Make a difference with, not for, students: A plea to researchers and reformers. *Educational Researcher, 24*(5), 12–17.

Corbett, D., & Wilson, B. (1997a). *Urban students' perspectives on middle school: The sixth grade year in five Philadelphia middle schools.* Philadelphia: Philadelphia Education Fund.

Corbett, D., & Wilson, B. (1997b). *Cracks in the classroom floor: The seventh grade year in five Philadelphia middle schools.* Philadelphia: Philadelphia Education Fund.

Corbett, D., & Wilson, B. (1998). Scaling within rather than scaling up: Implications from students' experiences in reforming urban middle schools. *The Urban Review, 30*(4), 261–93.

Corbett, D., Wilson, B., & Williams, B. (1999). *FY98 interim report: The*

129

second year of the assumptions, actions, and student performance OERI field-initiated study. Washington, D.C.: U.S. Department of Education.

Delpit, L. (1988). The silenced dialogue: Power and pedagogy in educating other people's children. *Harvard Educational Review, 58,* 280–98.

Elmore, R. (1996). Getting to scale with good educational practice. *Harvard Educational Review, 66*(1), 1–26.

Fordham, S., & Ogbu, J. (2000). Black students' school success: Coping with the burden of "acting white." In R. Arum and I. Beattie (eds.), *The structure of schooling: Readings in the sociology of education.* Mountain View, CA: Mayfield Publishing.

Fullan, M. (with S. Stiegelbauer). (1991). *The new meaning of educational change.* New York: Teachers College Press.

Furstenberg, F., Neild, R., & Weiss, C. (1999). *The Philadelphia education longitudinal study (PELS): Report on the transition to high school.* Philadelphia: Philadelphia Education Fund.

Hedges, L., & Nowell, A. (1999). Changes in the black-white gap in achievement test scores. *Sociology of Education, 72*(2), 111–35.

Heshusius, L. (1995). Listening to children: "What could we possibly have in common?" *Theory into Practice, 34*(2), 117–23.

Heubert, J., & Hauser, R. (eds.) (1999). *High stakes: Testing for tracking, promoting and graduation.* Washington, DC: National Academy Press.

Jackson, P. (1968). *Life in classrooms.* New York: Holt, Rinehart and Winston.

Jencks, C., & Phillips, M. (1998). *The black-white test score gap.* Washington, DC: Brookings Institution.

Koretz, D. (1992). What happened to test scores, and why. *Educational Measurement: Issues and Practice,* Winter, 7–11.

Koretz, D. (1995). Sometimes a cigar is only a cigar, and often a test is only a test. In D. Ravitch (Ed.), *Debating the future of American education: Do we need national standards and assessments?* Washington, DC: Brookings Institution.

Kozol, J. (1992). *Savage inequalities: Children in America's schools.* New York: Harper.

Kushman, J. (Ed.) (1997). *Look who's talking now: Student views of learning in restructuring schools.* Portland, OR: Northwest Regional Educational Laboratory.

Kusimo, P., Carter, C., & Keyes, M. (1999). I'd like to go to Harvard but I don't know where it is: Bridging the gap between dreams and reality for adolescent African American girls. Paper presented at the

Annual Meeting of the American Educational Research Association, Montreal.

Ladson-Billings, G. (1994). *Dreamkeepers: Successful teachers of African American children.* San Francisco: Jossey-Bass.

Luhm, T., Foley, E., & Corcoran, T. (1998). *The accountability system: Defining responsibility for student achievement.* Philadelphia: Consortium for Policy Research in Education.

MacIver, D., Plank, S., & Balfanz, R. (1997). *Working together to become proficient readers: Early impact of the Talent Development middle school's student team literature program. Report No. 15.* Baltimore, MD: Johns Hopkins University, Center for Research on the Education of Students Placed At Risk.

MacIver, D., Balfanz, R., & Plank, S. (1998). *The talent development middle school: An elective replacement approach to providing extra help in math—the CATAMA program. Report No. 21.* Baltimore, MD: Johns Hopkins University, Center for Research on the Education of Students Placed at Risk.

MacIver, D., Balfanz, R., & Prioleau, A. (1999). The fruit of looping: Impact on student motivation and achievement of assigning middle school teachers to the same students for two years. Paper presented at the Annual Meeting of the American Educational Research Association, Montreal.

Mezzacappa, D. (1996). Dreams of college meet dose of reality. *Philadelphia Inquirer,* February 25, A1.

Michie, G. (1999). *Holler if you hear me: The education of a teacher and his students.* New York: Teachers College Press.

Nieto, S. (1994). Lessons from students on creating a chance to dream. *Harvard Educational Review, 64*(4), 392–426.

Noddings, N. (1992). *The challenge to care in schools.* New York: Teachers College Press.

O'Connor, C. (1999). Race, class, and gender in America: Narratives of opportunity among low-income African American youths. *Sociology of Education, 72*(3), 137–57.

Ogbu, J. (1987). Variability in minority school performance: A problem in search of an explanation. *Anthropology and Education Quarterly, 18,* 312–34.

Oldfather, P. (1993). Students' perspectives on motivating experiences in literacy learning. *Perspectives in Reading Research,* No. 2, Summer. Athens: National Reading Research Center, Universities of Georgia and Maryland.

Oldfather, P., & West, J. (1999). *Learning through children's eyes: Social construction and the desire to learn.* Washington, DC: American Psychological Association.

Philadelphia School District. (1999). *Tell them we are rising—The Philadelphia story 1994–98: How Philadelphia schools are helping children achieve.* Philadelphia: The author.

Pitkiff, E. (1993). Teacher absenteeism: What administrators can do. *NASSP Bulletin, 77,* 39–45.

Pogrow, S. (1998). What is an exemplary program and why should anyone care? A reaction to Slavin and Klein. *Educational Researcher, 27*(7), 22–28.

Pogrow, S. (1999). Rejoinder: Consistent large gains and high levels of achievement are the best measures of program quality. *Educational Researcher, 28*(8), 24–26, 31.

Popham, J. (1998). Farewell, curriculum: Confessions of an assessment convert. *Phi Delta Kappan,* 380–84.

Popham, J. (1999). Why standardized tests don't measure educational quality. *Educational Leadership, 56*(6), 8–15.

Poplin, M., & Weeres, J. (1992). *Voices from the inside: A report on schooling from inside the classroom.* Claremont, CA: Claremont Graduate School, Institute for Education in Transformation.

Roderick, M., & Camburn, E. (1999). Risk and recovery from course failure in the early years of high school. *American Educational Research Journal, 36*(2), 303–43.

Ross, R. (1999). How class-size reduction harms kids in poor neighborhoods. *Education Week, 18*(37), 30,32.

Shields, P., & Knapp, M. (1997). The promise and limits of school-based reform: A national snapshot. *Phi Delta Kappan, 78*(4), 288–94.

Simon, E., Passantino, C., & Foley, E. (1998). *Making sense of standards: Children achieving and changing instructional practice.* Philadelphia: Consortium for Policy Research in Education.

Tomlinson, T. (1990). Class size and public policy: The plot thickens. *Contemporary Education, 62,* 17–23.

Wasley, P., Hampel, R., & Clark, R. (1997). *Kids and school reform.* San Francisco: Jossey-Bass.

Wiggins, G. (1999). *Assessing student performance: Exploring the purpose and limits of testing.* San Francisco: Jossey-Bass.

Williams, B. (1996). *Closing the achievement gap: A vision for changing beliefs and practices.* Alexandria, VA: Association for Supervision and Curriculum Development.

Wilson, B., & Corbett, D. (1999). *"No excuses": The eighth grade year in six Philadelphia middle schools.* Philadelphia: Philadelphia Education Fund.

Windschitl, M. (1999). The challenges of sustaining a constructivist classroom culture. *Phi Delta Kappan, 80*(10), 751–55.

Appendix
Student Interview Protocols

Year 1

We established these questions in conjunction with PEF and teachers in the schools. We were all in agreement that because the focus of the study was the effects of Children Achieving, we would limit topics to those related directly to school. Although the sets of questions are numbered below, the actual order in which we asked them depended on the course of the conversation with each student. Not all questions were asked of every student—due to the direction the interview took and time constraints.

1. What do you plan to do in terms of further schooling and in terms of work/career? Do you feel that this school is preparing you well to do that? Why? What happens here at school that is particularly helpful to your learning? What happens that is not particularly helpful? What else could the school be doing to help you with your plans?

2. What kinds of activities in class help you learn best? Why? Examples? Do you get to do these activities in all of your subjects or only in some? What kinds of activities in class do not help you learn? Why? Examples? What do teachers do that helps you learn? How does this help you learn? What could teachers do to help you learn more? Why? What opportunities do you have to work with computers or other technology?

3. Are you successful in school? Why? Is that your definition of success? What else does it take to succeed here? What is your teacher's definition of success? How do teachers let you know how well you are succeeding? Is this definition the one that should be expected of you? Why? Is it difficult or easy for you to be successful?

4. Do you feel safe at school? Why? Are there unsafe places at school? Do you have any suggestions on what else the school should be doing about safety?

5. What do you like best about being at this middle school? Why? What do you like least about being here? Why?

6. Do you feel like you are part of the school (that you are welcome)? What makes you feel welcome? What happens that makes you feel unwelcome? Do you have any concerns about coming to and being at school?

7. How often do you have homework? Do you usually do yours? Why? When do you tend to do it? What help do you have (who helps you) with your homework? Do you prepare for your classes and for tests? How do you do this?

8. How do you feel about school lunches? Why don't students eat them?

9. How easy was it for you to make the change from elementary to middle school? Why? How did you end up at [school]? Would you recommend this school to siblings/family?

10. Do you usually know how well you have done on a test or project before you received a grade or do you have to rely on the teacher to know how well you have done? How do your teachers figure out what grade to give you? Could you explain how your grade is determined in your favorite class? Your least favorite?

11. Who decides which activities you will do in your classes? Are you ever asked for your advice on what to do? Would you like more of these opportunities? Suggested activities that you would like to see in your classes?

12. Do you get much of a chance to be creative? Why? Examples? Would you like more opportunities to be creative? Why?

13. Are students treated fairly here? Why? What do students do that gets themselves in trouble? How are these problems handled? Is this the best way to handle them? What do students get praised for? Examples? Are there other things that students should get praised for?

14. What is your favorite class? Why? What activities do you like to do in this subject?

15. Are you involved in any extracurricular activities here? Which ones? Are there any other activities you would like to see offered that aren't?

16. Why do you think some students do not want to go to class? What can be done to change this?

17. Why do some students hang in the hallways? What can [school] do to help them?

18. How do students treat one another here? How can the school get students to show respect for one another?

Year 2

The above questions continued to set the broad parameters for interviews in the subsequent years. However, the primary purposes of the Year 2 and Year 3 interviews was to get the students to elaborate on themes we heard in the previous year and to have them update us on developments in the school that had changed. In the following list, the question(s) after the Roman numeral were guiding topics for us to keep in mind; the questions after the lowercase letters were the ones we actually asked.

I. Why do students report they are successful when indicators suggest they aren't? How do teachers' standards influence students' views of their performance?
    (a) What does it take to get an A in a particular class? (sample across major subjects)
    (b) What is the difference between an A and a C in that class?
    (c) A C and a F?
    (d) Is that true for all of your classes?
    (e) If not, what are some of the differences across classes?
    (f) What grades do you usually get?
    (g) Is it easy or difficult to get those grades?
    (h) How hard is it to get an A?
    (i) What subjects do you do research in when putting together projects or reports?
    (j) What are the steps you go through to put together your research project/report? (probe for putting information in their own words)
    (k) What kind of feedback do teachers give you on your research? (letter grades or comments)
    (l) Do teachers make you redo work that they say is not acceptable? How do you respond?

II. Why do students say they value education but don't behave accordingly?
    (a) Students say they value education, but few act like they want to be in school. Why?
    (b) What would it take for students to show more enthusiasm for school?
    (c) What sort of activities would really get your attention?
    (d) How do these activities help you learn better?

    (e) What do teachers need to do to make classes more interesting?

    (f) Can you tell me about some activities in your classes that really helped you learn?

III. Are the differences in instruction that students experience from class to class important?

    (a) Do students behave differently for different teachers? How and why?

    (b) Do you learn more in some classes than others?

    (c) How do you know you are learning more? Why?

    (d) How much of this difference depends on you and how much depends on the teacher?

    (e) What does the teacher do who helps you learn more?

IV. Why do so many students say they will attend college but few will likely do so?

    (a) Do you plan to go to college?

    (b) Why do you say this?

    (c) Do your teachers talk about students going to college?

    (d) How will college help you?

    (e) What will you need to do in school to be able to go to college?

    (f) How many people do you know who have gone to college?

    (g) What have they told you about college?

V. Do students value challenging work?

    (a) How do students react when the work in school is hard for them?

    (b) What kind of work is hard for you? (What does hard mean?) Why?

    (c) What do you do when the work gets hard? Why?

    (d) What should the teacher do to help you when the work is hard?

    (e) Do you prefer easy work or hard work? Why?

    (f) Do you like learning outside of school?

    (g) Is reading part of that learning?

    (h) How often do you read outside of school?

    (i) Where do you get your reading materials?

    (j) Is the school library a challenging/fun place to learn?

    (k) How often do you visit there?

    (l) What do you do when you are there?

    (m) Who do you go with?

    (n) Does the library have the materials you need?

Year 3

The final year's interviews followed up answers from the previous years. In most instances, we would begin the interview by reminding students of a couple of their prior answers and asking if those still were applicable. We had two other entry points to the conversation that we used: a general question about how things were going and a query about their future plans, since most of them were headed to high school. The interviews then, once again, took different directions. One addition we made to the interviews was to have students describe for us the routines in specific classes. Up to this point, we felt that we did not understand well enough what students thought went on in their major subjects. We used descriptions of the routine as the route to get them to elaborate on this topic.

I. How is school going this year?
    (a) Do you feel like you are getting a good education? Why?
    (b) How well prepared are you for high school? Why?
    (c) Has anything changed at this school during the three years you have been here? What?
    (d) What advice would you give for improving the school?

II. Tell us about specific classes this year? (probing for each subject separately)
    (a) What does your daily routine in _____ class look like? What activities do you do most often?
    (b) What activities help you best and how frequently do you do them?
    (c) How well are you doing (grades) this year? Do you understand how your grade is determined?
    (d) Are you learning new things or do your classes review things you have already learned?
    (e) Do you learn more in some classes than others? Why? Do you behave better for some teachers than others? Why?
    (f) What is your favorite class and why?
    (g) How do you know when you are doing well?
    (h) How do you define a good teacher?
    (i) Do you prefer when your teacher gives you challenging or easy work? What is challenging work for you?
    (j) Last year you said you preferred for your teachers to be strict. Do you still prefer that? In what ways are your teachers strict? Which ways work the best for you and your friends?

III. Future plans?
   (a) Where are you going to high school?
   (b) How did you decide about which high school to go to and where did you get information about the schools?
   (c) What role did your parents and teachers play in your high school selection?
   (d) What are your plans beyond high school? Why have you changed your plans (from previous years, if they have)?
   (e) Do you think you can get where you want to go with your current effort? Are you on the right track?
   (f) What might you have to do to make sure you can reach your goals?

Author Index

Subject Index

LISTENING TO URBAN KIDS

SUNY Series, Restructuring and School Change
H. Dickson Corbett and Betty Lou Whitford, editors